THE FAMILY DANCE

A Play

by

FELICITY BROWNE

SAMUEL

FRENCH

LONDON

NEW YORK TORONTO SYDNEY HOLLYWOOD

SAMUEL FRENCH LTD, 26 SOUTHAMPTON STREET, STRAND, LONDON WC2E 7JE, or their authorized agents, issue licences to amateurs to give performances of this play on payment of a fee. **The fee must be paid and the licence obtained before a performance is given.**

Licences are issued subject to the understanding that it shall be made clear in all advertising matter that the audience will witness an amateur performance; and that the names of the authors of the plays shall be included on all announcements and on all programmes.

The royalty fee indicated below is subject to contract and subject to variation at the sole discretion of Samuel French Ltd.

The publication of this play must not be taken to imply that it is necessarily available for performance by amateurs or professionals, either in the British Isles or overseas. Amateurs intending production must, in their own interests, make application to Samuel French Ltd or their authorized agents, for consent before starting rehearsals or booking a theatre or hall.

Basic fee for each and every performance by amateurs in the British Isles — Code M

In theatres or halls seating 600 or more the fee will be subject to negotiation.

In territories overseas the fee quoted above may not apply. Application must be made to our local authorized agents, or if there is no such agent, to Samuel French Ltd, London.

Applications to perform the play by professionals should be made to MARGARET RAMSAY LTD, 14A Goodwin's Court, London WC2.

ISBN 0 573 11124 3

MADE AND PRINTED IN GREAT BRITAIN BY
LATIMER TREND & COMPANY LTD PLYMOUTH

MADE IN ENGLAND

THE FAMILY DANCE

First presented by H. M. Tennent Ltd by arrangement with Donald Albery on June 5th, 1976, at the Criterion Theatre, London, with the following cast of characters:

Ben Musgrave	Alec McCowen
Toby Musgrave, his brother	Michael Bryant
Diana Verney, his sister	Helen Lindsay
Sophie Musgrave, his wife	Annette Crosbie
Victoria Musgrave, Toby's wife	Judy Parfitt
Charles Verney, Diana's brother-in-law	James Warwick
Michael Verney, Diana's husband	Anthony Nash

The Play directed by Jonathan Hales
Designed by Eileen Diss

The action takes place in the kitchen of the Musgraves' house

ACT I Late evening
ACT II A short while later

Time—the present

ACT I

A vast kitchen. Early evening

The ceiling is lost in darkness. There is an enormous deal table, covered with loaded plates; a large Aga cooker where the range once was; a towering dresser covered with plates and objects, with drawers underneath. Copper preserving-pans, etc., are hung on the wall. Various bits of non-kitchen furniture—tables, a piano, etc., have been stacked up in a corner, but the kitchen is so large they make little impression. A door leads to the rest of the house, another to the garden. An opening leads to the pantry

As the CURTAIN *rises voices are heard off, then a crash*

Ben (*off*) That is *enough*!
Toby (*off*) Diana said——
Ben (*off; cutting in*) Never mind.
Toby (*off*) But the sideboard . . .
Ben (*off*) I'm not moving anything else. (*Pause. In surprise*) There's Socrates. Who put Socrates here? (*Silence*) What's he doing here? (*Silence*) Oh, the whole house is upside down. Here. Give me a hand . . .
Toby (*off*) What with?
Ben (*off*) Socrates, of course.
Toby (*off*) Thought you weren't——
Ben (*off; cutting in*) Shut up! Take that end.
Toby (*off*) You're going to——
Ben (*off*) Who—ow!
Toby (*entering*) —scrape your knuckles.

Ben and Toby enter from the house, staggering under an enormous rocking-horse. Ben Musgrave is a square, powerful, volcanic figure, given to sudden outbursts. He puts far too much energy into everything, and looks as if he may burst out of his clothes. His hair is wild. He is aged about forty-five, and wears a dinner-jacket. Toby, his brother, is thin, looks pale, ill and gone to seed. He is elegant and, unlike Ben, looks good in his clothes. He is forty-ish and neat in his movements. He also is wearing a dinner-jacket

Ben puts his end down carefully, then examines his knuckles with passion, licking them

Ben Why didn't you *say* so?
Toby I just did.
Ben *Blood* poisoning . . . (*He goes to the sink to wash his hands*)

Toby From a wall?

Ben They're out of their minds.

Toby Who?

Ben Diana and Sophie. (*He explodes*) Don't they realize what sort of a week I've had? Don't they realize I need a rest to give me strength for Monday? (*Pause*) But what do I find? The house is to be packed with young people.

The sunset fades

Toby Your idea entirely.

Ben Young bloody people.

Toby "Let's all band together and give a dance for the children's friends." You said.

Ben Why do they have to be young here?

Toby One of your expansive days.

Ben Isn't Berkshire full of houses to be young in? Other people's houses?

Toby *You* wanted five hundred guests. *You* . . .

Ben (*turning on him*) Well? Isn't that what the house is for? Why do you think I keep on this blasted back-breaking millstone of a house, if it is not so that our-children-may-dance-in the rooms where their forebears danced?

Toby Bit of an anachronism, some might say.

Ben Anachronism? A vast pile like this where brothers and sisters and their husbands and wives and children co-exist in the warm, crowded atmosphere of a working-class slum? It's not an anachronism, it's dodo-land.

Toby All I was saying was that it's no use complaining about the guests when you invited them yourself. One hundred and fifty of them.

Ben What a good idea.

Toby But with refusals and chickenpox we're down to a paltry one hundred and twenty-five.

Ben I hope they're grateful. They—who's got chickenpox?

Toby All invited by you, so for once you cannot blame——

Ben I'm not having them here with chickenpox——

Toby —anyone else.

Ben —I might get it. Does *no-one* in this house consider me?

Toby Those with chicken-pox won't come.

Ben How do you know?

Toby They're in bed.

Ben No-one with spots is to cross the threshold. I forbid it. Examine them at the front door.

Toby How about acne?

Ben Acne?

Toby Endemic in that age group.

Ben (*jumping on Socrates and riding him furiously*) *No-one* considers me. My health. My well-being. My—happiness—are—of—no concern—to anyone—in this house. To hell with them. All. All. All.

Toby (*laughing excitedly while Ben rides*) Do you remember playing Greenmantle?

Ben slows down and stops entirely. He sits very still

Ben Greenmantle! "There is a dry wind blowing through the East, and the parched grasses await the spark. And the wind is blowing towards the Indian border. Whence comes that wind, think you?"

Toby (*very quietly*) "Where would you start the fire?"

Ben (*very quietly*) "Where the fuel is driest."

Toby (*very quietly*) "Sister Anne, Sister Anne, do you see anybody coming?"

Ben (*suddenly starting to propel Socrates, shouting*) Holy War! Holy War! Jehad! Jehad!

Toby (*seizing a chair and riding it backwards as if for chair-polo, shouting*) Peter's got through. The Russians are round the flank. The town is burning. Glory to God, we've won, we've won!

Ben The Cossacks! The Cossacks! God! How they're taking that slope! By Heaven, we'll ride with them! With them!

Toby Oh, well done our side!

Ben Ride knee to knee for the city!

Toby Ride for Erzerum!

Ben
Toby } Erzeru-u-um! { (*Shouting together*)

Socrates goes slower and slower, and finally stops

Ben A good ride. That was a good ride.

Toby You were ten. I was five. You were confined to barracks—the nursery—for disobedience. You wanted to go ratting with Gammel. You were furious—white and dangerous—as you rode for Erzerum. (*Pause*) You were always the most exciting person in the world.

Ben Me? My dear Toby, take another look. (*Silence*) I don't expect you've looked for years. There's nothing much left. (*Pause. He rides thoughtfully backwards and forwards*) Was it worth it? Was any of it worth it?

Toby Was what what?

Ben Oh—giving up my life—of which I had considerable hopes—to support this everlasting maw of a household. Are we happy?

Toby Happy.

Ben I thought we would be, you see. I thought that if, in a mad, shifting, intolerable world, we could all stay united in this house, then our children would have roots, and having been brought up together would support each other through life——

Toby Buckets along on his chair.

Ben —and I thought we would all contribute. But here's the rub. No-one, except me, works. And the burden of supporting this household is making me old and frantic. *You've* never had a job . . .

Toby I'm waiting . . .

Ben Waiting?

Toby (*rising from the chair*) Erzerum—Erzerum.

Ben Look, I'm *serious*. Then Diana—well, Diana marries a man who won't work . . .

Toby Michael's all right.

Ben Of course he's all right living off the fat of the land at my expense . . .
Toby He keeps Diana happy.
Ben (*ironically*) Oh good. And what about me? Who keeps me happy?
Toby Neither of us qualifies for married bliss.
Ben Victoria and you . . .
Toby Yes.
Ben Not the world's best marriage. Is it?
Toby Hardly.
Ben What . . .?
Toby I don't know. (*Pause*) Being unhappily married takes up such a lot of the day.
Ben And night.
Toby And night.
Ben Can't you . . .?
Toby Leave it, Ben.
Ben Why don't you . . .?
Toby Leave it.
Ben But surely you . . .
Toby Leave it. Leave it. Leave it.
Ben (*dismounting from the horse*) Oh Socrates, Socrates, what an ugly world. Only you are unchanged. How superb you look. Your nostrils are as red as ever, you look so young. (*Pause*) I'm old, Socrates. Old and frantic.
Toby (*lifting covers and inspecting dishes*) They'll never eat all this.
Ben Don't touch those plates.
Toby What will happen to their livers? (*Pause*) Why not?
Ben Because Diana will blame me.
Toby She's only our sister . . .
Ben The young don't have livers. They're slim and beautiful. They and Socrates.
Toby You scared? Of Diana?
Ben Of course not.
Toby I *am* surprised. Frightened of Diana. You.
Ben I don't like being blamed unfairly.
Toby I'll own up.
Ben I shall still be blamed.
Toby Why?
Ben Because I'm the oldest. The responsible one.
Toby Hardly relevant.
Ben Of course it's relevant.
Toby When you were five times as old as I was, yes. When you were twice as old, yes. But now? You're forty-five. I'm forty.
Ben It may not matter outside this house. But here—if you touch that ham—it's my fault.
Toby Oh, fiddle faddle, fiddle faddle. (*He strokes the horse's mane*)
Ben And stop pulling Socrates' mane.
Toby The rights of primogeniture don't extend to Socrates. He's as much mine and Diana's as yours.

Pause

Ben I'm afraid that's nonsense. Socrates belongs to me.
Toby Why?
Ben He always has. He's mine, that's why.
Toby Ours.
Ben Mine.

Pause

Toby Ours.

Diana Verney, their sister, enters from the house. She is in her early forties, built on a large scale, big head, big nose, big body, big feet, but very handsome. She has a loud, firm, not unattractive voice, an excellent carriage and considerable grace. She is dressed in splendid, conventional evening dress, bare-shouldered, and looks grand, terrific, beautiful and self-confident. No nonsense

Diana You're doing *nothing*—what are you thinking of?
Toby I say . . .
Diana Do you imagine we're ready? (*She takes a necklace from the dresser and puts it on*)
Toby Your best—once-a-year dress——
Diana That there's nothing to be done?
Toby —Balenciaga——
Ben —for an evening at the sink.
Toby Haven't you overdone it?
Diana (*taking an apron from a hook and putting it on*) How could I overdo it for the children's friends? Who could matter more?

Toby bows to her. She curtsies

Jane has toothache. Where are Sophie and Victoria? Why aren't they here? I can't bear it if her evening is ruined by toothache—I've given her salt and hot water—where *are* Sophie and Victoria?
Toby Haven't seen them.
Diana Well, why *not*, they're your wives. You all *knew* I had to go out all afternoon visiting Aunt Lalage, but it hasn't occurred to any of you to do anything helpful, and we're not nearly ready . . .
Toby If it comes to that, where's your husband?
Diana Michael? He's in bed . . .
Ben (*moving to go*) What an extraordinarily good idea and how stupid of me not to have thought of it myself. Luckily it's not too late.
Diana (*taking silver and two cloths out of a drawer*) Don't be silly, he's got 'flu. I told you before, but you never listen.
Ben (*exploding*) How am I to keep alive in a house seething with 'flu, acne, and chickenpox?
Diana Go to bed, indeed. We've only you and Toby left to dance with anyone who's left out.
Ben There's Charles.

Diana Charles won't help if it doesn't amuse him.
Toby Which it won't . . .
Diana (*giving Toby some spoons and two cloths*) Here, Toby, take these and give them a polish—we need every bit in the house.
Ben Am I to house not only my sister's husband, but my sister's husband's brother . . .
Diana He *is* your brother-in-law——
Ben He is not, he is *not*! He's *your* brother-in-law.

Toby puts one cloth in Ben's pocket

Diana —and families are the most important things in the world.
Ben To me he is my brother-in-law's brother, *not* a relationship where the majority would consider hospitality necessary——
Diana I've powdered Grizelda's spots—they hardly show. Did you move the sideboard?
Ben —but if I have to house him he can pull his weight and dance his legs off.
Diana The sideboard. (*She brings two lettuces from the pantry*)
Ben I've had enough of Charles. He makes trouble . . .
Toby Leave it, Ben.

Pause

Ben Why . . .
Toby Leave it.
Diana Can't you polish a bit quicker?
Ben And who does Socrates belong to?
Diana You *can't* leave the sideboard where it is.
Ben Tell Toby, will you?
Diana It takes up too much space, everyone will bump into it.
Ben Tell Toby.
Diana Tell him what?
Ben Who—Socrates—belongs to.
Diana Toby, of course.
Ben Nonsense.
Diana Don't be silly. He was a present from Toby's godfather.
Ben Socrates was here before Toby was born.
Diana Months before. Mother was very upset in case Toby was stillborn.
Toby Stillborn? Why should I be stillborn?
Ben But he's mine . . .
Toby Never had any intention of being stillborn. (*Pause*) I can see it would have solved a lot of problems. Shaving—marriage—whether to go to the movies or stay at home——
Ben He's always been mine.
Toby —not to mention disease, old age, and death.

Pause

Ben (*business-like*) How much will you take for him?

Pause

Toby He's not for sale.

Diana (*snatching the polishing-cloth from Toby in a fury*) Neither of you has any sense—don't you realize the *time*? The guests will be here . . .

Ben Why not?

Toby You can offer me nothing I want.

Ben You're short of money.

Toby Yes.

Ben In ever-increasing difficulties.

Toby Yes.

Ben Sell him.

Toby No.

Ben Swop.

Toby What for? Mess of pottage?

Ben I'm serious.

Toby Dust and ashes?

Ben What do you want?

Toby Thirty pieces of silver? Cloud-capped towers? Gorgeous palaces?

Ben You've been drinking. Already.

Toby The great globe itself? Or all the rights of primogeniture? (*Pause*) No.

Diana Oh, *stop it*, I'm ashamed of you both.

Ben But it's very important . . .

Diana To whom?

Ben Me. Of course.

Diana This is the children's evening. Not yours. They're going to remember this evening for the rest of their lives. Tonight they're going to make memories to warm their old age. Turn yourself outward, Ben. Think of them. And remember Sophie. (*She rummages in drawers and begins counting forks*) Look at these forks—Victoria promised to clean them.

Ben Sophie?

Diana Sophie.

Ben Oh yes, Sophie.

Diana You must know your wife's name after seventeen years.

Ben What's the matter with Sophie?

Diana Nothing. Until you upset her.

Ben Why should I?

Diana Because you always do. Eleven—twelve . . . She's perfectly all right during the week—useless about the house, of course, but quite *happy*. And then on Friday night you come back. Seventeen—eighteen . . . And then you do it. Every time. As you come through the door. If only she could shout back at you like the rest of us . . . Oh bother, Ben, you've made me lose count, how selfish you are. What are you *doing*, both of you? Nothing—nothing. Toby, get the candlesticks out.

Toby Where are they?

Diana (*indicating*) In that cupboard.

Toby runs to the cupboard and looks

She *could* shout back at you, you know. She's not frightened. Or weak.

Toby They're not here.

Diana Of course they are, why can't you *look*?

Ben She preserves her energy. For her painting. None of it comes my way. A mere husband.

Toby (*finding the candlesticks and bringing them to the table*) Here they are. Well done, Toby. I say, Diana, they're here. Look, here they are, I found them.

Ben Oh, stop chirruping.

Toby Why should she waste her energy on a monster?

Ben A *monster*?

Toby "If you look upon monsters, take care you do not become one yourself; for, should you gaze down into the abyss, the abyss may enter into you."

Ben (*struck*) That's good.

Toby Thank you. (*He sits and polishes*)

Diana I wish you'd both be quiet . . .

Ben Your own?

Toby Nietzsche.

Diana How can I count these forks?

Ben I like it. Say it again.

Toby If you look . . .

Diana No—no. *No.*

Ben Something the matter?

Diana She ought to leave you, really. I shall tell her so, I think.

Ben *What?*

Diana Not now, of course. I'll have a little talk with her tomorrow.

Silence

Ben I support this household.

Diana Michael . . .

Ben Yes, Michael contributes—but his books—what was the last one, *Golfing Tales of an Old Codger*, butter few parsnips.

Toby A rare phrase.

Ben I support this household. Slave for it—for all of you. I pay for every bloody thing—yes, I know Michael pays the subscription to *Country Life*, but I don't read it.

Toby Only I don't know what it means.

Ben Everything I pay for. Gin—roof repairs—cat food. And what do I get in return?

Toby Thanks.

Ben Thanks? *Thanks?* You're out of your mind.

Toby Praise.

Ben That's what a *normal* household would give for benefits received. But *you*? While I shorten my life with overwork, what happens? *What happens*, I ask you?

Diana (*bridling*) His books may not make much money but they get very good reviews.

Ben I will tell you what happens.

Toby Gratitude.

Ben My wife escapes if I come near her. My little brother turns the household into a public spectacle by getting indecently drunk—at my expense, naturally—in the middle of the afternoon on the village street—you thought I didn't know, you're mad, people flocked to tell me as I got off the train. Meanwhile, back at the happy home, my sister, whom I trusted, wants to persuade my wife to leave me . . .
Diana I don't expect to succeed.
Ben I should hope not. She knows which side her bread is buttered on—(*glaring at Toby*)—and so, may I say, do you.
Toby Gratitude. (*Pause*) And love.

Silence

Ben I didn't mean it. (*With passion*) I didn't mean it, I didn't mean it.

Sophie, Ben's wife, enters from the house. She is in her late thirties, fairish, thin and slight, dressed in paint-bespattered jeans and carrying a sketch-book and pencil. She often tries to sink into the background to avoid the noise of family life roaring round her; but her face is neither weak nor humble, and when she notices anything that interests her, light and life pour into it. All her attraction comes from these sudden glimpses of interior life. Unlike her husband and sisters-in-law, she is both quiet and still. Her movements when she is out of her element—i.e. doing any kind of kitchen job—are awkward. Diana would peel ten potatoes in the time Sophie would take to peel one

Diana Toby, why are you sitting down? You haven't finished . . .
Toby No?
Diana The coasters, look, they're filthy—and the candlesticks, you haven't done them, they're disgusting . . . (*She sees Sophie*) Good heavens, Sophie, don't you realize guests will be coming? What are you doing dressed like that?
Sophie (*looking down at herself, surprised*) I was working, I forgot.
Diana Working?
Sophie Painting.
Diana Oh, I thought you meant *working*, like the rest of us.
Sophie I'm sorry. I forgot.
Diana Forgot? Forgot the children's dance? I can't understand you, Sophie . . .
Sophie Something went right. It doesn't often. I didn't want to stop halfway.
Diana Then you didn't forget.
Sophie I suppose not. No. I didn't. But I'm here now. What would you like me to do?
Diana Where's my list? Ah. Do you think you can do salad dressing?
Sophie Of course.
Diana You ought really to be changing . . .
Sophie It takes me five minutes.

Sophie goes off to the pantry

Diana That's *much* better, Toby. Even Thwaites couldn't have polished them better.
Toby Well done, Toby, we knew you had it in you . . .
Diana Ben, I did ask you to move the sideboard.

Sophie enters with a tray on which are oil, vinegar, a pepper-mill and a basin, which she puts on the table, and sets to work

Ben You did, indeed.
Diana But it's still there.
Ben I struck.
Toby (*moving to the door*) Come on, Ben.
Ben Toady.

Ben and Toby exit to the house

Diana (*to Sophie*) What are you doing, dear?
Sophie The salad dressing. Like you said.
Diana But where's the lemon?
Sophie Lemon?
Diana We always use lemon in the salad dressing.
Sophie Oh. I didn't know.
Diana But we *always* use lemon. How could you not know?
Sophie I suppose I didn't notice.
Diana (*going to the pantry*) I wish you'd try not to be so dreamy. (*She returns with a lemon and a squeezer*) Really, it make me cross. How long have you been in this house?
Sophie Seventeen years.
Diana There. (*She gives her the lemon and squeezer*) Married to Ben for seventeen years. And you still haven't noticed that in *this* house we have lemon in the salad dressing. Oh Sophie, how *can* you not have noticed? How *can* you be so thoughtless?
Sophie It's not intentional . . .
Diana I never said it was, but it's very upsetting for everyone. I don't know why you do it.
Sophie I said. It's not intentional.
Diana You don't *try*, dear. (*Pause*) Sometimes I think you don't notice any of us.
Sophie (*stung*) Indeed I do. Look. (*She opens her sketch-book and shoves it under Diana's nose, turning the pages*) Look at that.
Diana Why, it's Victoria in one of her moods—when she can't get what she wants.
Sophie And that . . .
Diana Nicola running towards you—oh, that's really very amusing, it's *her*.
Sophie And that . . .
Diana That's—oh no, dear. Ben's not like that. You've made him so—threatening. And—looming. Why, you've made him into a monster, you know. How very odd that you should see him like that. (*Pause*)

After all, he is your husband. Now put it away, Sophie dear. Everyone will be arriving and nothing's ready. And do you know what Victoria's doing?

Sophie No.

Diana I'm *telling* you, dear. She's playing billiards with Charles. *Now*, of all times.

Ben and Toby enter. Toby goes to pour a drink

Sophie sits and mixes the dressing

Ben Another vertebra gone.

Diana Well done, Ben, that's very nice. Now what next . . . ? (*She looks at her list*) Yes. Toby, come with me and look *very* carefully to see nothing breakable has been left lying about. You too, Ben . . .

Ben No, it's rest hour.

Diana Then you can at least do something useful. (*She throws the polishing-cloth at him*)

Diana and Toby exit to the house

Silence

Sophie (*mumbling, head down over the dressing*) Had a good week?

Ben What?

Sophie (*more clearly*) I said, "Had a good week?"

Ben (*polishing forks*) I've been in the house for twenty-four hours. Why ask now?

Sophie Suppose we haven't seen each other much.

Ben When I came to bed you were asleep. When I woke up you'd gone. And I haven't seen you all day.

Sophie I've been painting.

Ben No doubt. But you can hardly blame me if we "haven't seen each other much".

Sophie I didn't . . .

Ben I'm sorry. I thought you did.

Silence

Ben } It never occurs to Diana that I need a rest at the week-end.
Sophie } The children are very excited.

They both stop

Sophie Sorry.

Ben Go on.

Sophie No, you go on.

Ben What did you say?

Sophie Oh, nothing . . .

Ben You did. You said something.

Sophie Nothing important. What did *you* say?

Ben Look, I asked you what *you* said.

Pause

Sophie I said, "The children are very excited". About the dance. (*Pause*) What did you say?

Ben (*slowly*) I said, "It never occurs to Diana that I need a rest at the week-end". (*He rises*)

Pause

Sophie Oh.

Ben So neither of us said anything. (*He cuts a slice of bread*)

Sophie Don't you think it's time we did?

Ben puts the bread in the toaster

Ben, I want a divorce.

Ben (*not listening*) No-one cares, of course, but I haven't had my tea.

Sophie Ben . . .

Ben (*rummaging in a cupboard for jam*) What is it?

Sophie I want a divorce.

Ben A divorce? Who from?

Sophie You, of course.

Ben Me? Don't be absurd. Of course you can't have a divorce. (*He brings the jam to the table*) What utter nonsense. Divorce me? What *for*, for heaven's sake? I'm the easiest man in the world to live with. *Divorce.* Good grief. We've been married for fifteen years.

Smoke begins to rise from the toaster

Sophie Seventeen. Seventeen years.

Ben Seventeen, then. Seventeen years. Well, you might as well stick it out to the end after seventeen years. (*He sits*) Do you know, I'm absolutely shocked. No, really, the more I think of it. And hurt. By *God* I'm hurt. I must say, Sophie, I'm very surprised. I . . .

Smoke pours from the toaster

(*Rising*) You bloody fool, you've burnt my toast . . . (*He throws the burnt toast into the sink*)

Sophie The thing's broken.

Ben Everything's bloody broken, oh, all the love in this house is flying out of the window.

Sophie I mean it, Ben.

Ben You break every bugger I buy—don't give them the slightest love and attention—of course they break.

Sophie You might just as well let me go.

Ben Your average toaster needs affection. Encouragement. Understanding.

Sophie We could both get a bit of peace.

Ben (*viciously*) *But you haven't any of that, have you?*

Sophie Any of what?

Ben Affection. Encouragement. Under-bloody-standing. (*He picks up the jam pot*)

Sophie You must see we'd be far better apart.

Ben (*conversationally, eating a spoonful of jam from the pot*) Frightfully good jam.

Sophie We'd both be so much happier——

Ben I suppose you didn't make it.

Sophie —saner——

Ben Bought at enormous cost from some blasted supermarket.

Sophie —have more chance of surviving . . .

Ben (*putting the jam down*) Divorce. Good God, what are you thinking about? Don't you realize marriage is for life? What about your vows?

Sophie Vows consistently broken carry little weight.

Pause

Ben What are you on about?

Sophie Who were you talking to on the telephone this morning?

Pause

Ben The garage.

Pause

Sophie The garage.

Ben The garage.

Sophie I *heard* you, Ben. I heard what you said. (*Pause*) Look, I don't know who she is and I don't really care . . .

Ben (*shouting*) Why not? Why don't you care? How dare you not care? (*More quietly*) Listening round corners. (*Shouting again*) It's *intolerable* the lack of trust in this house. Life's not worth living without trust.

Sophie That's what I'm saying. So let me go.

Ben Look. It's all right. I forgive you.

Sophie Let me go.

Ben I forgive you. (*Pause*) In any case I don't see why you should mind. Sex is hardly your strong point. You've never liked it——

Sophie I get so tired——

Ben —wanted it——

Sophie —and then you get so cross.

Ben —wanted me.

Silence

Sophie You know I bore you.

Ben You never *listen* to me—if only you'd listen . . .

Sophie I do listen.

Ben When I tell you which marmalade—which coffee—I like . . .

Sophie Oh—that.

Ben *That! That!* Are my tastes so irrelevant? My needs—my desires . . .

Sophie But I'm not good at——

Ben —listening. *Listening!*

Sophie I do listen. But you shout so—I have to protect myself.

Ben What from?

Sophie Noise. I don't know. I don't know.

Ben Am I *so* awful? *So* repulsive?
Sophie It's not—oh, sometimes it's almost all right.
Ben What is?
Sophie Us. Sometimes. When we both try—like that picnic last month.
Ben Great day that was.
Sophie We both enjoyed it.
Ben But I got stung by a wasp.
Sophie Then, of course, you screamed and yelled and it was over.
Ben Well, it hurt.
Sophie So we went home.
Ben Anyhow, the grass was damp.
Sophie But *before* . . .
Ben Before?
Sophie Before you were stung . . .
Ben What about it?
Sophie We were close.

Pause

Ben Yes.
Sophie Why?
Ben We're married, aren't we? Why shouldn't we be?
Sophie In that case, why aren't we more often? Oh, can't we learn?
Ben It's not a question of learning. All you have to do is relax and—*listen.* Not escape into a private world and shut me out. (*He looks in the refrigerator and takes out a bowl*) Ah, mulberries. (*He goes to the table with the bowl*) I think of you—when I first saw you. Skating. You looked so full of promise. Hopeful.
Sophie I liked skating.
Ben (*furiously*) I wanted you. I've always wanted you. But I've never got you.
Sophie We've had children.
Ben What holds you back? I can make other women melt. Why not you? Why? Why? Why? Why did you look so happy when you were skating? So full of life? It was a lie. *Why* don't you want *me*? Why don't you want me? (*He shakes her*)
Sophie (*after a pause*) I've never felt like that about anyone.
Ben *Skating!* (*Pause*) These mulberries have got mould.
Sophie That's not mould.
Ben Of course it is.
Sophie No.
Ben Look at it.
Sophie Yes, I know, but . . .
Ben I know mould when I see it.
Sophie No, it's duck stock.

Silence

Ben What?
Sophie It's duck stock.
Ben Duck?

Sophie I splashed it on to the mulberries. When I was putting it in the fridge.
Ben Duck stock.
Sophie I was helping Diana. I got most of it off.
Ben Most of it.
Sophie There's only one or two globules left——
Ben Globules.
Sophie —and they don't taste at all, because I've tried.

Ben pours the mulberries into the waste-bin

Ben No-one—no mulberry fancier—will say thank you for mulberries and fatty duck stock.
Sophie You only had to scoop it off. (*Pause*) And now you're cross.
Ben I'm not cross. Not at all. Just disappointed. I like mulberries. I was looking forward to them. (*Pause*) Just—disappointed. I suppose mulberries and fatty duck sauce was suggested by one of your frightful women's magazines. The Common Market touch, how to make your average Austrian at home.
Sophie Austria isn't in the Common Market.
Ben If you try serving it up to the French you'll be in trouble.
Sophie I've *told* you how it happened——
Ben If you imagine your average Frog is going to be gratified at a mixture of that nature, you're mistaken.
Sophie —but, as usual, you don't listen.
Ben It may be *Haute Cuisine* to you——
Sophie You just go on shouting——
Ben —but to them it's frankly *merde*.
Sophie —and shouting and *shouting* . . .
Ben Because you never *listen*. You never think about me. You burn my toast . . .
Sophie (*screaming*) Oh, get a new toaster.

Pause

Ben Why?

Pause. Sophie takes hold of herself

Sophie New ones—are quicker. Better. Faster.
Ben You think new ones are more electric. You imagine this one works partly by candlepower——
Sophie (*slowly*) Oh, how silly you can make me sound.
Ben —and it's the candles that cause the smoke.
Sophie How *silly*.

Silence. They look at each other

Couldn't *you* leave *me*? Me and the children? (*Pause*) In peace?
Ben (*amazed*) Don't be silly. I live here.

Diana enters from the house

Diana, talk to Sophie—she's out of her mind. She wants a divorce. From *me*. She's off her head.

Diana Ben, your *tie* . . .

Ben Will you *talk to her*.

Diana It's falling apart before the evening's begun.

Ben Diana . . .

Diana Not now, dear. It's the children's evening. You mustn't be selfish. Now come along and help Toby and me. And Sophie, go and change. It takes you more than five minutes, you know. You think you're very quick but you're not—you take just as long as the rest of us. (*She takes Ben's hand and pulls him out*) *What* a time to choose to have a nasty, selfish quarrel . . .

Diana and Ben exit to the house

Sophie, left alone, puts her head in her hands

Victoria comes in from the garden entrance, very fast. She is Toby's wife, beautiful and very alive, tall, dark and flashing. She is self-willed and strong-minded; not a comfortable or easy person to have around; not particularly nice but with generous moments and sometimes appreciative. She can turn a room black at the drop of a hat if things do not go exactly as she wants them to. She is sudden and graceful of movement; and beautifully dressed

Victoria I suppose she found the silver. (*Getting out cleaning things*) Hell. Of course she did. "Victoria promised to do it—and look—look" . . . What's the matter with you?

Sophie I've just asked Ben for a divorce.

Victoria (*interested, but not stopping work*) Why now? (*She sits at the table to polish forks*)

Sophie What do you mean?

Victoria Not worse, is it? Than it's ever been?

Sophie Yes. I'm more—frantic.

Victoria What an evening to choose. What did Diana say?

Sophie Just that.

Victoria And Ben?

Sophie Brushed it aside.

Victoria Of course. (*Pause*) You'll never get him to listen, you know. You can't win.

Sophie I must . . .

Victoria How can you? You've never been able to fight Ben. What makes you think you can begin now? After all those years?

Sophie I *must*. I'm swamped.

Victoria He'll walk over you. Like he always does.

Sophie If I can't get out I shall die.

Victoria He won't oppose you. He won't hear. It's not worth trying.

Sophie I *must*.

Victoria (*after a pause*) You're not going to anyone else, are you? (*She cleans the silver rapidly and noisily, not looking up*)

Sophie Only to myself. Back to myself.

Victoria Is it worth it? Why upset things?

Sophie I've told you. Because I shall die if I don't get away.

Victoria *Die?* Don't be absurd. (*Her eye is caught by the sketch on the table. With an exclamation of fury*) Why do you always draw me looking like that?

Sophie Like what?

Victoria Like—like *that.*

Sophie (*gazing at the drawing, lost in thought, forgetting Victoria*) Is it too—implacable? (*Pause*) The single-minded pursuit of self-interest . . .

Victoria (*outraged*) Sophie!

Sophie (*coming to*) I'm sorry, I'm *really* sorry, I didn't mean anything, it was just an—an aspect of you that interested me . . . Oh, please don't quarrel, I couldn't stand it with Diana's dance looming over us . . .

Victoria *Diana's* dance—whose house is this?

Sophie Ben's.

Victoria Who is Ben's wife?

Sophie Oh, I know, but . . .

Victoria It's *your* dance—*your* house—why is everything always Diana's?

Sophie The house belongs to Diana because she fills it. It's hers by natural right. (*Exclaiming*) Of course it's not *my* house, when even the noise of family life exhausts me.

Victoria Noise? What noise?

Sophie Oh, the thundering clash of ego bouncing off ego. And no-one in this house ever talks. They all roar and yell . . .

Victoria I'd never noticed. Do they? We?

Sophie All I want—all I ever hope for—is time for work and then to get through the day quietly. No trouble. No noise.

Victoria A modest wish.

Sophie But seldom, if ever, realized.

Diana enters from the house, running

Diana (*to Victoria*) You haven't cleaned . . .

Victoria I have. I have! Look! Glowing! (*She holds bits up*)

Diana Well, you hadn't done it twenty minutes ago.

Victoria Ah, but I have now.

Diana Yes, dear, but you shouldn't leave things until the last minute.

Victoria Why not?

Diana It's a mistake, that's why. Sophie, you haven't changed yet.

Sophie (*rising*) Oh—I'll go and do it now.

Sophie, muttering, exits to the house

Victoria (*to Diana*) How grand you look—lacking only long white gloves . . . (*She rises*)

Diana (*perfectly seriously*) No, I've got them. Of course.

Victoria I *don't* believe it. (*She puts the cloth away*)

Diana (*producing the gloves*) Of course I have. Full evening dress means long white gloves.

Victoria Meant. In the days of the Romans.

Diana Romans?

Victoria Oh, don't you remember the Romans? Who ruled our childhood and straightened our backs? The nannies, oh and the great-aunts, what great-aunts there used to be. But they're a long time gone, taking with them their long white gloves, and their cucumber sandwiches—their croquet mallets, their leather-bound prayer-books, their . . .

Diana I'm sure it's very clever, dear, but I don't know what you're talking about.

Victoria You don't find it at all odd dressing up with long white gloves to pass an evening washing-up in the kitchen? Because that's what we'll be doing.

Diana It's the *principle*, dear.

Victoria Wouldn't jeans and an apron be more in keeping?

Diana Of course not. We're having a dance.

Victoria The *children* are having a dance—we're doing the washing-up—fetching and carrying. We ought to be dressed as maids, flunkeys . . .

Diana Yes, dear, very nice.

Victoria You're not listening.

Diana Victoria, could you stop Toby drinking? Just for this evening?

Victoria How?

Diana Well, talk to him. (*She puts the salad dressing on the refrigerator*)

Victoria What good will that do?

Diana You're his wife. You ought to be able to stop him—it's absurd that you can't put your foot down.

Victoria Toby would agree with everything I said. Then he'd go off and drink the same as usual. So why waste breath?

Diana If you weren't so careful with your breath Toby might be happier—you don't give him enough, love, that's the trouble.

Sophie enters wearing a Jean Muir dress

I don't think you try very hard. (*She examines Sophie*) There you are, dear. You're rather—covered up, aren't you? I mean, it's a very nice dress, but no-one would guess you had a good figure, really you're quite *hidden*. And the colour is somehow—the same colour as the rest of you.

Victoria Sophie isn't beige. (*The colour must depend on the available dress—but the word describing it should be evocative, funny or strange*)

Diana Don't be silly, Victoria, of course she isn't. But her hair's pale and her face is pale and so is her dress. Perhaps if we pinned a rose on her . . .

Victoria No.

Diana Yes, look—I'll just find a pin. (*She rummages in a drawer*)

Victoria No. It's wrong.

Diana It will make all the difference.

Victoria It will look macabre.
Diana Macabre, really, Victoria . . .
Sophie Oh, can't you both stop shouting over me?
Victoria Shouting?
Diana Don't be silly, dear. We're helping you. You don't want to look drab, do you? (*Shutting the drawer, and sighting the carving-knife*) Who on earth put the carving-knife *here*?
Sophie I did.
Diana But it's the wrong place. *This* is where the carving-knife goes. (*She moves it. Pause*) Fancy you not knowing that.
Victoria The carving-knife belongs wherever Sophie puts it.
Diana What, dear?
Victoria It's *her* house. Not yours. Not mine. Hers.
Sophie Oh, please . . .
Diana Of course, Victoria. We all know that. But there's still a right and wrong place for a carving-knife. The right place is here. In this drawer. Ah. Here's a pin. (*She pins a rose on Sophie*) There. (*Pause*) Oh dear, it doesn't . . . Never mind. It's better. (*Pause*) I *think* it's better. (*Pause*) Perhaps a belt . . . No. Well, never mind, dear, you have such nice eyes. Now—I must go and receive the guests.
Victoria (*emphatically*) That's Sophie's place.
Sophie (*quietly but intensely*) Oh Victoria, please, *please*.

Ben enters from the house

Ben (*to Sophie*) Why are you wearing that rose?

Diana seizes Ben and makes him waltz

It looks dreadful.
Diana Oh Ben, how silly you are.
Ben Diana, tell her to take it off.

Sophie exits to the house

As Ben and Diana dance round the room they duck whenever they reach a certain spot

Why was Sophie wearing that appalling rose? That dress needs nothing —it's marvellous. (*Duck*)
Diana *Marvellous?*
Victoria You're ducking.
Ben Of course. Hadn't you noticed?
Diana But it's so drab.
Ben My dear Diana, you don't know *anything*. (*Duck*)
Victoria Why are you ducking?
Diana I gave her the rose. I thought the dress needed cheering up.
Ben Cheering up? Diana, you're unbelievable. (*Duck*)
Victoria What—are—you—ducking—for?
Diana (*to Victoria, plonking*) To avoid the hams, of course.

Victoria What hams? There aren't any hams.
Ben A dreadful, blowzy rose——
Diana (*plonking*) No, but there used to be, dear. Of course.
Ben —in the middle of that perfect dress . . .
Victoria How many years ago?
Diana Years ago?
Victoria Since there were hams? Really, this house is absurd—don't you realize? The shibboleths—no-one must sit in this chair because Annie died in it . . .
Diana Don't be silly, Victoria. *That's* the chair Annie died in.
Victoria Then this is the one James used to rest his gouty foot on, so that's sacred too.
Diana I hope you're not being funny about poor James. He suffered a great deal.
Victoria In every corner of the house there's a private god.
Ben (*sitting down*) I'm not enjoying myself. What is Sophie on about?
Victoria She wants to leave you.
Ben *Why?*
Victoria For peace. Quiet. Time to work.
Ben But she *can't* want to leave me—not seriously. Why?

Toby enters from the house

Victoria Perhaps it's no fun.
Ben Fun! How silly. How frivolous. I'm going to bring her to her senses. And she can begin by taking that rose off.

Ben exits to the house

Diana (*going after him*) Leave her *alone*, Ben. Ben, leave her *alone*.

Diana exits

Silence. Victoria starts washing lettuces

Toby Well. Here we are. In a room together. Alone. (*Silence*) A rare occurrence. Happening seldom by day. Never by night. As you like it, I suppose. As you like it.
Victoria A great year for slugs.
Toby If only I could fancy someone else. Ideal solution. But from the moment I saw you you filled my heart and my mind and my eyes, and will do until my last breath. (*Silence*)

"If any beauty I desired and got
'Twas but a dream of thee."

Do you remember how happy we set out to be? In another world.

Silence

Victoria The aphids, too, are doing well.

Toby If you would only tell me in what way I—displease you, perhaps I could do something about it. (*Silence*) No. I've frozen you up just by talking about it. Let's put it away again. (*He opens a drawer*) There, creepy-crawly. In you go. (*He slams the drawer shut*) And stay there. (*Pause*) How right you are to find talking a bore. A mouth opening and shutting. What's the use, you say. And how right you are. As always. Always right, my wife. (*Pause. Briskly*) Well now, what's left? (*He pours himself a whisky*)

Victoria Do you really want another whisky?

Toby Do I want another whisky? Do I want another whisky? Well, do you know, I rather think I do. (*Pause*) Do you mind?

Victoria It's nothing to me.

Toby Yes, I know.

Victoria For the sake of the children you might try and stay sober——

Toby Ah! The children's dance!

Victoria —just for once.

Toby Supposing we were to meet this evening for the first time—no past——

Victoria I imagine they would prefer it.

Toby —I would have a fresh start with you——

Victoria Although I expect they're so used to it that it's a matter of indifference to them——

Toby —and, I suppose, fail again.

Victoria —as it is to me.

Silence

Toby Some of those children—now fresh, unscarred—will meet their Waterloo on that dance floor tonight. As I did when I first saw you.

Victoria (*ironically*) You wish to call off the dance.

Toby (*after a pause*, *quietly*) Yes. I do wish to call off the dance. But it's in motion. Unstoppable. (*He shivers*) But who wouldn't call it off, call it all off, if he could?

Victoria Anyone willing to accept a few scars.

Toby My marks and scars I carry with me. My sword I give . . . No. Nothing to do with me. I have not lived bravely. I have ducked at the sight of trouble and legged it from the field of battle. At the sound of the trumpet I have buried my head beneath my pillow. (*Pause*) I can feel you sneering. But you were born brave. What merit is there in that? (*Silence*) With you, speech is superfluous.

Diana enters from the house

Victoria is growing bored at the thought of the guests——

Victoria (*without interest*) Toby, you're behaving like a fool.

Toby —and so am I. We've all heard too much about them. Let's call the whole thing off.

Diana (*to Victoria*) Can't you stop him drinking? Just for this evening?

Victoria (*as a statement*) How can I.

Toby You may address me, you know. I am here. (*Looking in the glass*)

"Among those present was debonair Toby Musgrave." (*Pause*) In hell.

Diana picks up the coasters and candlesticks. She speaks to Victoria hurriedly and quietly, but Toby overhears

Diana Why don't you do something? Why do you care so little?

Toby (*pouring another drink*) Just what I always say myself. (*Pause*) You realize we're not a stable enough household to have a children's dance? There are too many echoes, undertones, overtones. The guests will be embarrassed and want to go home.

Diana Toby, I hope you're not going to get the horrors again tonight. It's very upsetting for the rest of us. (*She goes to the door*) Do you hear, Toby? No horrors.

Diana exits, and Victoria follows

Ben (*off*) Nothing to do with me is important, we all know that. First thing we learn in this house.

Sophie (*off*, *exhausted*) I've said I'm sorry. You'd better take this one as well, Ben. I just forgot.

Toby takes another whisky, and holds the glass to Socrates' mouth

Ben enters with some letters

Ben (*as he enters*) Leave me alone. Leave me alone. Stop following me about. Under her bloody paintings. My whole week's post.

Toby Socrates was thirsty. (*Pause*)

Ben Why won't you sell him?

Toby Don't want to.

Pause

Ben Why?

Toby Don't care. (*He does a drunken dance to the tune of "I Won't Dance"*)
"Why should I?
I don't care
How could I?
I won't care
Merci beaucoup."

Ben No sense in being flippant.

Toby No sense in being serious. No sense. No sense anywhere.

Ben Rubbish.

Toby *Oh*. Oho. You think sense is about somewhere, do you? Where? Where? Lurking in the subterranean corners of the mind? Come out of there, sense, we know you're in there.

Ben Oh, don't be ridiculous.

Toby Aha. You think it's in the world about us. Outside. Exterior to the mind. But where? Under the table, perhaps. (*He gets down on all fours and crawls under the table*) Nothing there. Only a half-chewed bone.

(*Pause. He reappears with the bone*) Wonder if it's mine. Hope not. Let me see. (*He sits on the floor and takes off his shoes and socks, beginning to count his toes*)

Ben You're drunk. Again.

Toby Drunk or sober, my dear chap, I've got to make sure I'm all there.

Ben Oh, pull yourself together.

Toby Be reasonable, Ben, I can hardly do that before I know whether there's any of me missing. (*He goes back to his toes*) Eight, nine, ten. All present and correct. Spectacles, testicles, wallet and watch. (*Feeling himself, and getting it in the wrong order*) No, no. Spectacles, testicles, wallet and watch. (*He gets it right*) Yes. Right.

Ben Do get *up*.

Toby (*rising*) I wonder whose bone that was? One of the guests, perhaps. We must watch out for someone dancing a toe short. (*He mimes a man dancing in agony minus a toe*)

The telephone rings. Toby dances through the door to answer it in the passage

(*On the phone*) Hullo . . . No. None of us is here. I haven't seen any of us for days. Can't remember when I last saw us. (*He slams the receiver down*)

Ben I suppose you realize that might have been for me? That it might have been important? The way you behave is *intolerable*.

Toby *My* behaviour intolerable, good grief, what about you? Filling the house with people whose bones drop off.

Ben (*opening his letters*) This should have been answered days ago.

Toby *And* furthermore, when they've dropped off do they tidy them away? Call for a dustpan and brush? Not your guests. Just leave them lying about under the kitchen table, where anyone might fall over them, and where they constitute, no doubt, a considerable health hazard. Litter louts. That's the class of person you ask to the house. (*He goes to the door, staggering rather, opens it, and goes out, shouting at the top of his voice*) KEEP—BRITAIN—TIDY!

Toby is immediately pushed back into the room by Diana, who enters and shuts the door hastily

Just before the door closes there is a loud noise of guests arriving

Diana Oh, Toby, you *must not*, not this evening. (*She goes to the sink and washes some watercress*)

Ben sits and reads his letters

Toby Now don't sidetrack me. I was helping Ben—who has his troubles like the rest of us—to look for sense. He's lost it and I was helping him. Fraternal solidarity. I'd tried under the table . . .

Diana (*taking napkins off various dishes, garnishing the ham with the water-cress, etc.*) Don't be silly, Toby. You know perfectly well you won't find sense lying about under the table.

Toby Aha. *I* know that. Of course. You know it. But Ben doesn't. We've just got to ease him along. (*He sings*)

"Ease him along,
Singing a song,
Side by side."

(*He tiptoes over to Ben and bellows in his ear*) I'm with you, Ben!

Ben (*leaping up furiously*) Get out! Get out of my house.

Diana Don't be silly, Ben. He's your brother.

Ben Other people don't support their brothers. Other people's brothers grow up.

Diana That's not the point.

Ben What *is* the point? He gives me no pleasure. I don't enjoy having him around. I ought to get rid of the lot of you.

Toby Ah. That's what I say. Get rid of the lot.

Ben Do you think I wanted to spend my life like this?

Toby Get the decorators in.

Ben I'm fed up with the life I lead in this house. I pay for everything. All the burden falls on me. Money goes like water—and what do I get in return?

Diana I always think it's such a pity you're a stockbroker.

Ben (*unable to believe his ears*) Didn't you hear what I said?

Diana (*placidly*) Yes, dear, of course. (*Pause*) I just think it's such a pity you're a stockbroker.

Ben collapses

And I do wish, Ben, that you wouldn't talk about money all the time. You know we weren't allowed to mention it when Mother was alive, and now you never stop. She'd be very shocked, you know. Really I don't know what she'd say. (*Briskly*) In any case, you're being very silly because you know you couldn't do without us.

Ben Oh, couldn't I?

Diana You? Do without the children?

Ben Don't talk to me about the children. They've been screaming about the house all day. I haven't had a moment's peace—my eardrums are at risk.

Diana What a pity you've grown so old——

Ben They've been behaving——

Diana —in a childish manner. Like children. At the thought of a dance their hearts have risen. They don't know what's coming, but they expect *everything*—every unknown pleasure in the world. (*She glares at Ben. Pause*) How childish of their hearts to rise so lightly. In a childish manner, sillily.

Silence. Ben kisses her hand

Toby (*climbing up on the dresser and opening a cupboard above it*) The difference the decorators would make in this house; they'd throw everything away—everything. Look—Jacobean candle-snuffers—snuff—snuff—snuff. We even have an elephant gun, though I haven't seen many elephants lately—not in Berkshire—not at large. Look at all this junk. Look . . .

Diana What?

Toby pulls out a 1930s portable wireless from the cupboard. They all gaze at it

Good heavens. Nanny's old portable.

Toby You see? *Nothing* in this house gets thrown away.

Diana Things often come in handy.

Toby "Monday Night at Eight."

Diana Oh! The week's high spot.

Toby When Nanny used to bring her portable into the night nursery——

Diana —if we'd been good all week.

Toby She used to stretch it, though. She was decent. Always a helping hand from Nanny. (*Pause*) Why isn't she still around?

Ben gives an exclamation of disgust, Toby jumps down and puts the radio on the table

It's all very well for you to sneer. She could always cope with everything I couldn't learn—tying my shoes—dressing—keeping me tidy. If only, instead of being spent on useless expensive schools, the money had gone on providing me with a first-rate Nanny on a life contract. "Now come along, Master Toby, there's a good boy. Will you have another whisky if Nanny pours it for you? There it goes—down the little red lane."

Ben I *cannot believe* that all I deserve from life is to have Toby infesting my house, wearing my clothes, drinking my drink, and drooling on about Nanny.

Toby (*singing affectedly*) "It's Monday night at eight o'clock
Oh, can't you hear the chimes
They're telling you to take an easy chair
And settle by your fireside
Look at your *Radio Times*
For Monday Night at Eight is on the air."

Diana Oh, do you remember the game? Nanny was keen on that.

Toby "Guess what, guess why, guess the who and how
Of the things we'll ask you now—
Get your pencils and your paper out
You're the winner if you know about
Who the what the where the why and when
Which and wherefore and how now,
Which and wherefore and how."

Ben You've carried that inane drivel in your mind for over thirty years. How I'd hate to see the inside of your head.

Toby *Who* is Ben? *What* does he want? *When* did he turn sour? *Wherefore* is he desperate? *What does he want?*

Silence

Ben You can't play that game, little brother. You haven't got the courage. Or the energy.

Pause

Toby No. You're right. (*He pours himself another whisky*) Everyone in this house is right. Except me. Take my wife. Never stops being right. And Diana. Always at it. Even Ben has an occasional stab at it. Rightness is all.

Charles enters from the house. He is Michael's brother, amusing, light-weight, stylish, an easy talker, very social. He is much younger than his brother, and is wearing a dinner-jacket

Before Charles shuts the door loud music is heard

Charles Michael's shouting for you.
Diana Oh, I promised to take his temperature.

Diana rushes out

Ben (*shouting after her*) Can't he even lift a thermometer?
Toby The dance floor red in tooth and claw, where those who have are given abundantly more, and those who have not lose even that which they had.
Ben (*to Toby*) If you've got a memory like that, why don't you do something useful with it? Get a job?

Charles laughs

(*Menacingly*) Yes? Did something amuse you? Something about my brother, perhaps?
Charles Always good for a laugh, you and Toby, to a simple outsider like myself.

Pause

Ben Outsider.
Toby You're being too modest. You play quite a role in our lives. Wouldn't you say so, Ben?
Ben Considerable.
Toby Our brother-in-law's brother—almost a relation.
Ben A figure on the periphery of family life.
Toby Oh, closer in, closer in.
Ben You're right.
Toby Periphery means edge.
Ben An ill-chosen word.
Toby Yes. Nearer home than that, isn't he?
Charles That will do.
Ben Much nearer.
Toby Close?
Ben Very close.
Toby In a position of trust and affection?
Charles I said that will do.
Ben That's right.
Toby Trust.

Charles I'm not going to spoil Diana's evening by having a fight with you two.

Ben Fight? My dear fellow, you know how we love having you here—proud to have you in the family.

Toby We consider you an asset.

Ben And then, you make such a difference to Victoria.

Toby Victoria. My wife.

Charles Rotten games you two play.

Ben He says we play rotten games. I wonder what he means?

Toby Too clever for me.

Ben Our games rotten—what about yours? Cuckoo in the nest—that's your game.

Charles If it weren't for Diana . . .

Ben You'd do what?

Charles (*to Ben*) I'd knock your head off. (*To Toby*) Both your heads.

Ben (*savagely*) Adding physical assault to treachery.

Toby I *said* we shouldn't have a children's party.

Charles (*to Ben*) So shut up.

Toby Poor little perishers.

Ben You're in no position to tell me to shut up.

Toby Headless hosts.

Charles I'm telling you all the same—whatever my position.

Charles goes out, furious

The music is heard, wilder, until he shuts the door

Toby Areas of treachery and counter-treachery are best left unexplored.

Ben Rubbish.

Toby What do you gain?

Ben My feelings are relieved.

Toby (*pouring himself a glass of water*) Let's just leave it lying quietly. I don't wish to lose what little I still have of my wife.

Ben How can you be so feeble . . . ?

Toby A little is better than nothing.

Ben Is it?

Toby I console myself.

Ben With whisky.

Toby Well, that. But I say to myself either—you don't get what you want, or you get it. But when you do, it's probably too late. In either case, there's nothing you can do. So why worry?

Ben But you used to have hopes.

Diana enters

Music is heard

Diana Did we really ask as many as that? There seem to be hundreds of them. What a lovely noise they're making, and it's hardly started. Now, Ben, you take one of the heavy trays—I've got the children lined up to take everything from you.

Ben Come on, Toby. (*He picks up a tray*)
Diana Remember, no children in the kitchen.

Ben exits

(*Calling after him*) No children in the kitchen!
Ben (*off*) NO CHILDREN IN THE KITCHEN!
Diana Tell them to put everything with the rest of the food in the dining-room. Sophie! Victoria! Come and help.

Toby picks up a tray

Charles! No, Toby, not that one, dear, you're not very steady on your feet, you know.

Toby puts the tray down and picks up a plate of ham

Ben enters, followed by Sophie and Victoria

Ben They're all covered in spots.
Diana Ah, Sophie, you take the duck, and see that the napkins are on the table, will you, dear? There you are, Victoria, you take the pudding trolley and tell the children not to put the puddings on the table, they'll make marks.

Sophie exits with the duck, Victoria wheels off the trolley

Where is Charles? Why isn't he helping?
Ben (*shouting off*) Charles!
Diana (*calling after Victoria*) Oh, and Victoria, leave the trolley in there to bring things back on. Ben, you take the chicken-and-tongue. Has Nicola put the hamster away?
Ben I'll tell her.

Ben exits with the dish of chicken-and-tongue

Diana (*calling after Ben*) He'll be trodden underfoot.
Ben (*off*) Nicola, put that bloody hamster to bed. I know he's lovely, darling, but he can't dance.

Sophie enters and picks up another tray of food

Diana (*to Sophie*) Did Toby drop anything?
Sophie No.
Diana Oh, good.

Sophie exits. Toby enters

Oh, there you are, Toby. Well done. Now you take in the bread—*carefully*, dear.

Toby exits with an armful of loaves, picking up his glass of whisky and the bone on the way

(*Looking round and checking*) Rice, salad, silver—now is that really everything? (*She ticks off her list*) Yes, yes, yes. There, the kitchen's empty again.

Toby enters, shutting the door

Oh, Toby, what marvellous times we had in here when we were children. Do you remember how lovely and noisy it was? It was all such fun.

Toby Everyone loved us.

Diana *Was* it such a golden world?

Toby Oh yes, yes. Don't you remember?

Diana I think I do. But am I exaggerating? Life isn't really like that.

Toby It was—it was—you can't have forgotten.

Diana I do remember noticing things . . .

Toby Things?

Diana Like Mrs Eppings telling lies.

Toby *Lies?* Mrs *Eppings*? How can you talk like that?

Diana She did, Toby.

Toby Nonsense—she was as honest as the day.

Diana She was a hypocritical old baggage who cheated Mother over the housekeeping for years—and as for James, I always think he hated the lot of us . . .

Toby *Diana*—stop it—stop it . . .

Diana Good heavens, Toby, whatever is it? You're shaking. (*Pause*) What on earth does it matter now? They've all been dead for years and we're middle-aged . . .

Toby I don't believe it—I don't believe any of it.

Diana But it doesn't matter.

Toby Of course it matters.

Diana But they're all dead . . .

Toby They're more alive to me than anyone I meet in the street.

Diana (*not listening*) Do you remember how I used to dance on the table? After kitchen tea?

Toby "The table's clear, Miss Diana—get up and give us a dance."

Diana It must be thirty years since I danced on that table—thirty years good heavens, I'm forty-two. Oh, how *can* I be forty-two?

Pause

Toby Get up.

Diana Oh, don't be absurd.

Toby Get up.

Diana I can't.

Toby Go on.

Diana I can't.

Toby Please—come on.

Diana climbs up on the table

Diana Absurd. Oh. (*In surprise*) Everything looks different.

Toby You've grown.

Diana Yes, of course, so I have. (*Pause. She points at spaces round the table*) That was Annie's place—James—Mrs Eppings, Mrs Eppings, let me see, who sat next to Mrs Eppings?
Toby Thwaites. Of course.
Diana Of course. Then—Jenny—Martha—(*pause*)—oh, Toby, isn't it empty? It's so quiet . . .

Toby goes to the piano and starts to play a jig

Toby Of course it's nonsense. About Mrs Eppings and James. But I wish you hadn't said it.
Diana (*listening to the music*) Oh—that jig—what's it called?
Toby *Rory O'More*. Of course.
Diana Of *course*. Annie's favourite. But there's no-one to stamp, and no-one to shout—no-one to tell me I'm pretty . . .
Toby Dance to their memory.

Diana begins to dance

Ben bursts in while Diana is dancing

There is a discordant noise from outside before he shuts the door

Ben Are you mad? Good grief, you weigh a ton, get down before you break the table.

Toby plays a dissonant chord

(*To Toby*) What are you looking at me like that for?

Pause. Diana gets down from the table

Who has to buy a new table when Two-Ton Tessie has fragmented it? She's no slip of a girl.
Toby She was. For a moment.
Diana (*pushing past Ben*) He's quite right, Toby. I was being childish.

Diana exits

Ben (*gazing at the door*) What was that about? (*Pause*) Have I done something awful?
Toby How can you care so little? (*He leaves the piano*)
Ben But I do care.
Toby Then why don't you *look*?
Ben What have I done?
Toby Just for a moment—Diana was light of heart. Like she used to be. You put the years back on——
Ben Oh God . . .
Toby —and added some.
Ben Why didn't you warn me?
Toby Why didn't you look?
Ben (*roaring and bellowing*) Hell! (*He moves to the stove and fills a saucepan with hot water from the kettle on the Aga*)

Toby What are you doing?
Ben Boiling myself an egg. Food is the only answer to the strain of life in this house. I want—a boiled egg. (*He settles at the table with bread and knife, and cuts thin strips of bread with great concentration*)

Toby also settles at the table and watches him. Silence

Toby Bread and butter fingers. (*Silence*) You should butter the bread before you cut it. (*Silence*) *Everyone* knows that. (*Silence*) And you're cutting it too thin. It'll break when you dip it. (*He picks up a bit of the bread and waves it*) Poor, weak, wobbly thing. Pathetic.

Ben glares at him, and begins tearing off thick strips of bread with his fingers

Tearing the loaf apart. What would Nanny say?

The water boils. Ben puts an egg in the saucepan and looks carefully at his watch

Sophie enters

Sophie Would you like me to do that?
Ben You? And have it turn out like my egg this morning? What am I saying—"this morning"? Every bloody morning. All I ask is a fresh egg lightly boiled. So that when I dip my bread and butter fingers . . .

Toby snorts

Did you say something?
Toby No.
Ben (*glaring at him*) Where was I?
Toby Dipping your bread and butter fingers into your lightly boiled egg.
Ben Ah. There's the crux. They stub their toe on it. (*He goes to the dresser for salt and pepper*) Why? Because the bloody thing is solid. Iron hard every time. (*Pause*) Now you may think, "What is he making a fuss about? All he has to do is mention in passing to his loving wife that he likes his egg boiled for four-and-a-half minutes precisely, and Bob's your bleeding uncle—a perfect egg every time." But how wrong you would be. I have told *my wife* on an average of twice a week for the last seventeen years, and she *never gets the bugger right*. Seventeen years of spoilt eggs. (*He takes a plate, puts a hunk of bread on it, and then some butter*)
Toby (*going for another drink*) But you keep on at her, don't you? At her, at her, at her.
Ben (*to Sophie*) Just for once I am going to have an egg which is a pleasure to eat. So I am cooking it myself.
Sophie I hope you enjoy it.
Ben And do you know *why* you are incapable of cooking me a decent egg? Because you are not prepared to give a moment's thought to my needs, fears, tastes or desires. I might as well be in China for all you care. You're not prepared to do *anything*. You won't cook, you won't make

a bed and *neither will you lie in it*. Look at you now—you're not listening, you're not *listening*. What are you looking at?

Sophie I was looking——

Ben Yes?

Sophie —at that bread.

Ben Aha! The bread.

Sophie Who tore it into chunks?

Ben Ah!

Sophie Not that it matters.

Ben Oh, but it does. You find it disgusting.

Sophie I said it doesn't matter.

Ben You wish to begin at the other end. With a knife. Cutting delicate, even, artistic slices. Ha. (*Menacing her*) But what is going to happen when we meet in the middle? Eh, Mrs Musgrave?

Sophie stands facing him

Had you thought of that? (*Pause. He pulls off a chunk of bread and hands it to her*) Look. Have some with me. It's an eat-in, baby, a love-in. I have a mouthful. You have a mouthful. It's what it's all about. Bread. It's always been like that. Two people breaking bread together.

Sophie stands there

Oh, hell! (*He hurls the loaf on the floor, scattering the pieces, then suddenly remembers and looks at his watch*) *You bloody fool*, you've spoilt my egg *again!* (*He burns himself as he takes out the egg*) Ooow!

Ben gathers the whole lot on a tray and rushes out, leaving the door open

Loud music and laughter are heard until Toby shuts the door. Then absolute silence

Toby Drink?

Pause

Sophie What?

Toby Have a drink.

Sophie No. (*Hurriedly*) Why won't he let me go?

Toby Whisky? Have a whisky.

Sophie It's just as awful for him.

Toby (*pouring a whisky*) Do have a whisky.

Sophie But he can't let me go.

Toby *I'm* going to have one.

Sophie And I can't get away—can't get away anywhere. No refuge. No peace.

Toby Come and watch the children. We'll have a dance.

Sophie There may be a way to escape, but I can't see it.

Toby Are you all right . . .?

Sophie I can't see anything.

Toby fills his glass and goes

Sophie sits at the table, motionless

Diana comes in in a rush

Sophie starts

Diana . . .

Diana Where did I put it? How silly I am. I had it here. I put it down in a safe place. Oh, where did I put it? (*She searches around*)

Sophie When you tell me to leave Ben—where could I go? Can you think where I could go?

Diana Do help, Sophie, where's my car key? I've left my car in the drive and people keep on nearly bumping into it. What's that bread doing on the floor?

Sophie Where, Diana? Where? How do people do it? I'm such a fool. *How do people leave people?*

Diana I know it was a safe place—I can remember saying so as I put it down. To myself.

Sophie Diana, can you hear? How do people leave people?

Diana Not aloud. I didn't say it aloud. I was . . . Of course—the silver drawer. (*She opens the silver drawer and finds her key*) Of course—it's all right, Sophie, you can stop looking.

Diana rushes out

Sophie (*staring at nothing, quietly, dispassionately*) No-one. Nowhere. Nothing. No-one. (*Pause. She is suddenly galvanized, rises, goes to the dresser for the note-pad, writes on it, then props it on the kitchen table*)

Sophie goes to the door to the house, opens it and exits

Long pause

Victoria and Ben enter from the house; Ben carrying his tray. They are quarrelling

Victoria What do you mean, perhaps he's had the taste to leave the house? What do you mean?

Ben (*putting the tray by the sink and hurling the remains of his egg into the waste-bin*) *Another* uneatable egg!

Victoria Was there a quarrel? What have you done to Charles?

Ben I'm starving. No-one cares.

Victoria What happened to Charles?

Ben (*looking straight at her*) He was made aware that your husband and I were both cognizant of the blatant and unseemly manner in which the two of you have been comporting yourselves under my roof while enjoying my hospitality.

Victoria (*sitting down with a thump*) He's gone . . .

Ben No such luck. I should be delighted if you both went, but Charles would never take you on as a permanency.

Victoria Say he hasn't gone . . .
Ben Has he asked you to run away with him? (*Silence*) Of course he hasn't. Why should he, when he can have you here whenever he wants you at no trouble or expense, and leave when he gets bored?

Silence

Victoria He hasn't gone? Not gone? Say he hasn't gone.
Ben He'll be having a walk. Working out how to stay here without losing face. Then he'll come in and say to Diana, "What can I do to help you? Let me dance with the left-out ones—let me take that tray up to Michael—you're doing too much." He'll be helpful, thoughtful, kind. Make Diana grateful. Make her laugh. Then he'll be able to tell himself—and you—that although it goes against the grain to stay in the house of anyone as unmannerly as myself, unfortunately his sister-in-law needs him so much that he has no alternative but to put up with it. (*Silence*) You have nothing to say.
Victoria What can I say?
Ben Nothing?
Victoria It's true.
Ben No alleviating circumstances?
Victoria No.
Ben No comforting lies?
Victoria None. Except that if Toby had got away from this house he might have grown up—been different. We might have been—all right. When I married him I meant to be true, loving and faithful until death.
Ben We all meant something like that.
Victoria It might have been all right. Unless Charles had come along, of course.
Ben Why did you pick on that toadying lightweight? He's so boring.
Victoria Is he? I hadn't noticed.
Ben You've nothing in common——
Victoria (*suddenly*, *violently*) —except entrails. (*Silence*) Entrails, intertwined, and writhing. (*Pause. She continues conversationally*) You say he's boring. I daresay. I haven't noticed. I'm not interested in his mind.

Ben lifts his eyes to heaven

Why do you sneer? How dare you sneer? How dare you pretend that you don't know about this—this *condition*—when I've seen you white and sick with it? You, you, you yourself. (*Pause*) I've known you for thirteen years. I know you really quite well. And I've *seen* you, Ben. I've seen you after Dan Fielding's wife. I've seen you after the woman over at Lacklands—*prancing*. I've seen you—insane of this, this love-*disease*. You of all people know that it's like scarlet fever or measles—no-one can be blamed for catching it.
Ben I daresay. But it's ludicrous, it's embarrassing, it's——
Victoria —not nice. Not nice at all. A bitch on heat. (*She turns on him*) But it's surprised *you* before, hasn't it? Hasn't it? And may do again. (*Pause*) A gentleman surprised by passion. Deranged. Off the rails.

I'm—off the rails, Ben. Quite—off the rails. I might do anything. (*She exclaims*) Husband? Children? I've no time for them. They're—in my way. They stand between me and the light. Charles is the light.

Silence

Ben I'm sorry.
Victoria (*ironically*) Oh, thank you, thank you.
Ben Hang on. That's all you can do. Hang on and wait for old age. It'll pass.
Victoria *Pass?*
Ben Well, it never lasts, does it?
Victoria Of course it will last.
Ben But . . .
Victoria What?
Ben Look around you.
Victoria What at?
Ben Other people who've—caught it. Last year's passion this year is—spent?
Victoria Oh, yes, but that's other people. (*Pause*) This is different.
Ben Different?
Victoria Permanent.

Silence

Ben How can you believe that?
Victoria (*surprised*) Because it's true.
Ben But it doesn't last for anyone else—why should it last for you?
Victoria Because it's different.
Ben You're about forty. In ten years' time you'll be fifty. I haven't met many fifty-year-olds lately who were burning for anyone. There may be one or two. But sixty-year-olds?
Victoria If I were ninety-five my stomach would rise up and hit my heart when he came near. It's a diseased condition——
Ben —which you embrace.

Pause

Victoria Yes—it shows me things I'd never seen.
Ben Things? What things?
Victoria Lights—colours—the world. Just the world. Just the *whole* world. (*Pause*) I think I should die if it happened all the time. I quite often feel—since Charles came—that I may just die. Just—die. (*Silence*) What *is* all that bread doing?
Ben Signposting another failure of a husband and wife to behave towards each other rationally, kindly, or with love. (*Silence. He starts rummaging in a cupboard*) I need food. Ah. (*He produces a packet and studies it*) Cheese. (*Pause*) Christ—listen to this. In French, of course, the language of seduction and general carry-on. "It charms the palate—applies itself to pleasing you—seduces the most discriminating gourmets." (*He hurls the packet on the ground*) I don't ask much. But I do prefer a little reticence from my cheese. Is that unreasonable? Asking

too much? Why didn't Sophie buy a quiet, well-behaved chunk of Canadian Cheddar? One of the old school, trained like a Roman, never to show emotion, never to flinch? *I will not have* cheeses slavering all over me—guttersnipe, pariah, mongrel, *foreign* cheese.

Victoria reads the note, and rises

Victoria Sophie . . .
Ben And I daresay it was very expensive.
Victoria Ben——
Ben What?
Victoria Sophie——
Ben What about her?
Victoria She's taken an overdose.

CURTAIN

ACT II

The same. A short while later

When the CURTAIN *rises Ben and Diana are lugging the unconscious Sophie round the kitchen table. Victoria is making coffee. Toby, glass in hand, is sitting on the horse; throughout the following he rocks gently, never taking his eyes off Sophie*

Diana I know Sophie is often rather thoughtless, but this is the limit.
Ben We *must* get the doctor.
Diana She's just not trying.
Ben Don't you realize she may die?
Diana So like her not to exert herself.
Ben Supposing she dies?
Diana She always has time for that painting of hers—*work*, she calls it——
Ben Supposing she dies?
Diana —but ask her to do anything that *normal* people call work, and it's quite a different story. (*Briskly*) Come along now, Sophie. It won't do, you know, dear. You're not helping very much, are you?
Ben Diana . . .
Diana Yes, Ben, what is it?
Ben Will you *listen*?
Diana I am listening, dear, don't be silly.
Ben Supposing she . . .
Diana Anyone would think I'm the sort of person who never listens.
Ben (*shouting*) Supposing she *dies! Dies! Dies!*
Diana There's no need to shout.
Ben *Answer*, then!
Diana Of course she won't die. She was very clever and brought it all up.

Ben looks nauseated

Ben Then why does she look so—so—dead? Ugh . . .
Diana She's doing splendidly.
Ben Oh, right as rain.
Diana Don't fuss so, Ben. She's got to exert herself a little, to—to—come back.
Ben If only the doctor . . .
Diana Once and for all, Ben, I am *not* having doctors and ambulances in the middle of the children's dance. Don't be absurd.

Victoria examines a picture on the window-sill

Ben But Sophie——

Diana —has been a very silly girl, but now she's going to pull herself together.
Ben But . . .
Diana *No.*

They glare at each other over Sophie's inanimate form

Ben She is my wife.
Diana This is no time to think about yourself, Ben. Try and think about Sophie for a change.
Ben Good God, what do you think I . . .
Diana (*interrupting*) She needs a little coffee, that's all. Where is it, Victoria, isn't it ready yet?

Pause. Victoria still examines the picture

Victoria.
Victoria Mm? Oh yes—here it is. (*She pours out a cup and hands it to Diana*)
Diana That's far too hot, Victoria, do try and have a little sense. We don't want to give her a nasty burn, do we?
Victoria I'll blow on it. (*She goes back to the picture*) This is—extra-ordinary.
Diana What is? Oh, that. That's only one of Sophie's little things.
Victoria (*still studying it*) It's amazing.
Diana Amazing? It's only a tree.
Victoria Only a tree. But I'd never seen it before.
Diana Don't be absurd, Victoria. You see that tree every day of your life. It's the elm at the bottom of the kitchen garden.
Victoria I know *that*. But look—look, what Sophie's seen. She's seen it—for the first time, that tree. She's showing it to us—for the first time.
Diana I can't say I admire it. It's too empty.
Victoria Empty?
Diana If only she'd put one of the dogs in. Brutus would have looked very nice.
Victoria Lifting his leg, I suppose.
Diana Don't be vulgar, Victoria. Or perhaps one of the children—yes, Emma in her red sweater. That's it. Painters always like a touch of red in a composition. For a splash of colour. A focus, they call it.
Victoria What absolute nonsense.
Diana Excuse me, Victoria, but I do know about these things. After all, I was at school with Dora Chillick.

Pause

Victoria Who's she?
Diana You've never heard of Dora Chillick?
Victoria Never.
Diana But she's so well known. She exhibits at the Royal Academy quite regularly. I mean, her paintings *sell.*
Victoria And she always has a splash of colour?
Diana Oh, always. That's why her paintings sell so well. And of course, having been at school with her, I know all about it.

Victoria Why?

Diana Don't be silly, Victoria, it seeped into me. These things do if you let them. Like lovely music.

Silence. Victoria looks intently at the painting. Suddenly she turns to Sophie —urgent, urgent

Victoria Sophie, come back—come back. How *can* you give up? We need you—to show us. Don't take your eyes away—come back. Come back.

Ben Thank you, Victoria. I'm glad someone's got the point.

Toby still rocks gently, his eyes on Sophie as she is walked round the table

Toby Is she there? Are you sure she's there?

Ben What do you mean?

Toby Can she hear? Can she think? Can she speak? Or is there—nothing there?

Diana Of course she's there, Toby. Don't be ridiculous.

Toby All right, all right, don't snap my head off. All I'm saying is that she doesn't appear to be with us. Giving in fact, a remarkable imitation of an absent friend. (*He raises his glass*) Absent friends, and God save us all.

Diana Oh, stop it, Toby.

Toby Yes, but there's her *mind*, you see. Not here—not there—then where?

Diana You can come down off Socrates and have some coffee, Toby. You and Victoria are going to have to take your turn at walking Sophie, and I'd rather you didn't fall over.

Toby (*coming down and pouring coffee*)

We seek her here
We seek her there
We seek her almost everywhere.
Is she in heaven?
Is she in hell—
Or is she just a whippoorwill?

Ben We can't leave her with Toby in this state.

Diana We must, Ben. We can't desert the children altogether. Anything may happen. Are you all right, Toby?

Toby Right as a trivet. Merry as—as a——(*he frowns and sways*)

Ben We've been going round this table for fifty minutes. Supposing every one of those minutes was vital. Supposing . . .

Toby *—lark.*

Diana (*interrupting*) Look, she brought it all up, it's all *right*. Come on, Toby, we're changing over. Now, Victoria, you take my side.

Diana passes her side of Sophie to Victoria; Ben passes his over to Toby

(*To Victoria*) We'll be back in a minute as long as the children are happy. Just keep her walking.

Diana goes out to the house

Ben follows her to the door, then turns and puts out a tentative hand to Sophie

Ben Oh, *hell* . . .

Ben exits

Victoria and Toby stand still for a second, holding Sophie. Victoria looks anxiously at Toby as they start walking

Victoria You are all right, Toby? You won't suddenly fall over?

Toby It would take a far more determined character than I am to stay drunk in circumstances like these.

They walk Sophie round in silence

Victoria (*stopping*) We could try the coffee. (*She sits with Sophie below the table*)

Between them, they get the cup to Sophie's lips; she makes a choking noise

Toby Well, she's in there somewhere.

Victoria Why?

Toby She choked.

Victoria You don't think it was a—death rattle?

Toby Oh Lord . . .

Victoria I'm frightened. Are you?

Toby Petrified.

Victoria (*shouting*) Sophie—Sophie—do come back. Look, Diana says you're perfectly all right, and you *know* she's never wrong. So you've got to come back, you haven't any choice. (*Pause*) Diana—says—you're—all right. (*Pause*) Oh, don't be *silly*, Sophie, it's only this morning you had your hair washed. You can't die on the day you had your hair washed, it's absurd. (*Pause. Firmly*) Sophie. Sophie. I'm getting rather angry. We want you to have coffee with us. (*Pause*) Sophie—Sophie—you're being very selfish. (*Pause. She begins to cry*) You're making me cry, blast you.

Toby (*proffering his handkerchief*) Nerves.

Victoria What?

Toby Making you cry. Nerves.

Victoria I don't care what it is. I don't like it. Oh, come back, you silly girl, how can you be so *stupid*? Look—look at that tree. (*She pulls Sophie round so that if she were conscious she would be looking at the tree drawing*) *You* drew it—you *saw* it. Look—look at the life streaming out of it. How dare you try and kill yourself when you know about that life—look how sacred it is. How cowardly, how feeble—how *dare* you? Come back! Come back at once!

Michael Verney, Diana's husband, enters from the house. He is about ten years older than Diana. At the moment he is bowed down with 'flu and self-pity, and is wearing an ancient and disreputable dressing-gown

Toby Michael, Sophie's . . .

Michael Diana promised me coffee an hour and a half ago. (*He makes* *for the coffee and pours himself a cup*) Coming to something if a man with 'flu can't have a cup of coffee. (*Pause*) Sophie had one over the eight? More your line, Toby.

Victoria She's taken an overdose.

Michael Overdose, eh? Very impetuous. (*He makes for the door*)

Victoria Michael, don't you care at all?

Michael Care? What about?

Victoria (*furiously*) Sophie!

Michael Sophie? (*Pause*) Oh, you mean the overdose. She won't bring it off. Not Sophie. She'll have got the dose wrong. Anyhow, I daresay Diana's taken her in hand. Hasn't she?

Victoria Yes, but . . .

Michael There you are, then. Anyone Diana takes in hand is bound to be all right. She'll be as merry as a cricket in an hour or so. Well, I'm off to bed. Got to be careful. Don't want a cold on top of this 'flu.

Michael exits

Silence. Victoria talks to Sophie calmly

Victoria Did you hear that? Michael says you're perfectly all right. You're just being rather silly and obstinate. (*She turns on Toby in a sudden fury*) If only you weren't so drunk and ineffectual you'd—you'd—*do* something!

Toby What?

Victoria *Something!*

Pause

Toby Cold water on her forehead?

Victoria That's no good.

Toby Anything's worth a try.

Victoria Oh, all right.

Toby fetches a mug of water from the sink and splashes some on Sophie's face

(*with intense excitement*) Toby—Toby—did you see?

Toby She nearly spoke.

Victoria Didn't she? Didn't she?

Toby I *think* she's . . .

Victoria More water. (*Silence*) No. She's gone again. But she was *here*—just for a moment.

Toby Did you see her eyes?

Victoria Yes. There was life in them. Oh, what a relief, Toby, and it was all your idea. How clever of you.

Silence

Toby I can't remember how long it is since you've spoken to me like that. As though I were—a human being. You spoke—to me. (*Silence*) Yes. Well. One of those flukes.

He lifts Sophie. They start walking her round again

(*After a pause*) Victoria, if I—got a job—did something—would you be —pleased?

Victoria You're always talking about getting a job.

Toby But if I did—would you be with me? (*Silence*) You can't answer that. Don't try.

Diana and Ben enter

Diana (*to Sophie*) Not still being *silly*, dear?

Victoria It's all right—she nearly came to. There was a distinct flicker.

Diana Flicker?

Victoria Of life.

Ben You're sure?

Victoria Oh yes.

Ben Quite sure?

Victoria Yes.

Ben So she's perfectly all right.

Diana What are you talking about, Ben? I keep on telling you Sophie's all right. She's just being rather obstinate and unhelpful, but then of course, she always was.

Ben (*furiously, glaring at Sophie*) There's no need to speak of her in the past. She'll live to exercise her maladress for many years to come.

Diana Ben! Only a few minutes ago you were in such a state about her——

Ben —when I thought she was in danger of dying unshriven of this appalling sin.

Victoria Sin? You can't call Sophie trying to kill herself *sin*.

Ben Of course it's sin. In my canon, Dante's and God's——

Toby —in ascending order of merit.

Diana Really, Ben.

Ben What do you mean, "Really, Ben"? Can't I mention God?

Diana It's not Sunday, dear.

Toby sits Sophie and sits by her. Diana fetches a cloth and places it under Sophie's head

Ben Do you realize that under Queen Victoria attempted suicide carried the death penalty? Try and slit your throat and fail, and you were patched up quick as lightning so they could hang you.

Victoria You're being nauseating, Ben. (*To herself*) I wish Charles was here.

Diana Sin, indeed. Poor Sophie.

Victoria I think I'll just see if he's back.

Victoria exits to the house

Diana You're talking absolute nonsense, Ben.

Ben Oh, can't you see? *Why* can't you see? Suicide is despair. Which is sin. It is violence. Violence against the soul. And this too is—sin.

Toby You're using rather odd words, Ben. They don't mean much, you know. Not to most people.

Ben What does that matter, if they are true?

Toby I can't myself blame anyone for fancying a little oblivion.

Ben Oblivion? *Oblivion?* Who can guarantee oblivion? (*Silence*) Supposing she were to wake up to everlasting life?

Diana I wish you wouldn't talk like that, dear. It's not very nice.

Ben And supposing that when she woke to everlasting life she found herself carrying with her everything she was running from? The intolerable burden of her sins?

Toby Myself, I believe in a dead end——

Ben I wouldn't like to bet on it.

Toby —where at least she would have escaped from you.

Ben I wouldn't bet on that, either.

Pause

Toby Supposing you go on doing it.

Diana Doing it?

Toby Throw yourself off a roof—and you keep on doing it—every second—through eternity. Slit your throat—again and again and again. The same hesitation as you feel the razor's edge.

Diana Really, Toby, where do you get your nasty morbid ideas?

Ben He got that one from Dante. Who said it better. (*He shouts in Sophie's ear*) Are you listening? You're *very lucky* that this cowardly attempt of yours has failed. Because if you had succeeded and this theory were true you would be in for a very unpleasant time and I would not be in your shoes for all the money you might care to offer me. (*In a matter-of-fact tone*) Or for all the tea in China, as they say. (*He paces*)

Diana You were too much for her, Ben. You must try and be a little kinder. She couldn't stand it any more and suddenly something snapped . . .

Ben (*stopping in exasperation*) "Suddenly something snapped." I like that. Alliterative. Terse. Apposite. Above all, original. You must say it more often. A jewelled phrase like that deserves frequent airing.

Diana Don't you feel any pity for her?

Ben No, I do not. Fury is what I feel. A deep and passionate anger. Did she give a moment's thought to anyone but herself? To her children? Her husband? Her friends? No—no—*no* is the answer!

Diana There's no need to shout.

Ben There's too much of it about. You see it all the time—a little unhappiness, a modicum of domestic discontent, not getting entirely your own way, and it's on with the gas—head in the oven—down with the pills, a quick bit of wrist-slitting and hey presto, another opter-out has slipped his—or her—collar, his mortal coil, and sneaked out of the back door, leaving those behind bereaved, bewildered, and overwhelmed with useless, life-destroying guilt. I hate suicide. Also I think it's ineffectual. Useless. Because I believe in eternal life, and if eternal life exists then we must—answer. All of us. One by one.

Silence

Diana Really, Ben, you can't have it both ways. If sin and eternal life and—so forth and so forth—are true, then so are love and compassion, and you haven't shown Sophie the faintest glimmerings of either. And although she's been, very thoughtless in her choice of an evening—I hope you're listening, Sophie dear—it's entirely due to you that we have this lifeless object on our hands while the children dance.

Ben (*shouting*) I will not shoulder *everything* in this house! I will not pay all the bills *and* be blamed when the toaster breaks *and* when Sophie tries to kill herself! And what does she mean by doing it without telling me? She's got a tongue in her head. She might have mentioned it in passing.

Diana Oh, she did mention it, dear. Now and then over the past seventeen years. Most days, really.

Ben She moaned a bit . . .

Diana We've all told you for years. But you just went on talking.

Ben If my wife is going to commit suicide I expect her to mention it in passing. Over the toast and marmalade. While cleaning her teeth. Heavens, surely she can find a moment? (*Pause*) Why today, for heaven's sake? Nothing happened . . .

Toby What about the telephone call?

Ben What telephone call?

Toby The telephone call she overheard.

Ben Who told you about that? Did she?

Diana No-one had to tell us. You were shouting about it. Everyone in the house knows.

Toby You may not realize it, but you lack reticence.

Ben But that was totally unimportant.

Toby To whom?

Ben To me, of course.

Diana But not to her.

Ben It's no use making frivolous excuses for her. She's done this because she neither feared God nor loved man. And when she comes to I am going to teach her at least to fear God.

Toby (*going to the whisky*) Between fear of God and terror of you she won't know where to turn. (*He pours a drink*)

Ben There will be no repetition of this nonsense. She can stick it out to the end like the rest of us. (*Pause. To Sophie*) Do you hear? You can stick it out to the end like the rest of us!

Diana (*to Toby*) Oh Toby, not *another* . . .

Toby (*mounting the horse*) Another. And another. And another. But I'm like Sophie. No short cut to oblivion.

Ben Oblivion is not to be had so easily.

Toby That had not escaped me. But I keep on trying. Battle of Britain spirit.

Victoria enters

Victoria He's *nowhere*.

Diana Who?

Ben (*exasperated*) My dear Diana . . .

Victoria I've looked all over the house.

Diana What's she talking about?

Ben How naïve you are.
Toby Charles. She's talking about Charles.
Victoria It's not like him . . .
Ben He'll be back. Comfortable house. Easy living.

Ben lifts Sophie, Diana goes to her other side

God, she's getting heavy. This'll ruin my back. When she comes to she can go on a diet.
Diana Don't be silly. She's as light as a feather.
Ben (*shouting at Sophie*) Do you hear? You can go on a diet and get some of that weight off.

Diana and Ben start walking Sophie round again

And I'm hungry. (*Pause*) I suppose your husband has dined. He knows how to look after himself.
Diana You're not to be horrid about Michael.
Ben I have the deepest respect for your husband, and unqualified admiration for the way he avoids anything unpleasant by going to bed and staying there until the all clear.
Diana He's very delicate.
Ben School sports, boring neighbours, the children's dance—he can always run up a temporary illness which never stops him eating or drinking and provides you with healthy exercise running up and downstairs with trays. I hold no brief for the generally held theory that he's a fool.
Diana He's not.
Ben I agree. He's a very clever man. And he got his supper tonight, unlike the rest of us.
Diana You're being . . .
Ben Didn't he?
Diana Certainly I took him up a little liver. He needs it.
Ben *And* a little strengthening claret?
Diana Do you grudge him a glass of wine?
Ben A *glass*?
Diana There's no sense in keeping an open bottle until the next day.
Ben My best Château Léoville-Poyferré, I suppose. No, I'm not complaining. I'm only asking what there is for us?

Pause

Diana Sausage rolls.

Silence

Ben (*very quietly*) Sausage rolls. How are we to support an abortive suicide on sausage rolls?
Toby Had Diana known that Sophie was going to try and do away with herself the knowledge would no doubt have been reflected in the menu.
Ben She could have guessed that *something* would go wrong. It always does, after all. It happened to be Sophie, but it might have been you drunk and insulting the guests, or fire breaking out—but it is always something. This is not a house where you can afford to serve sausage

rolls *at any time*. Because here stomachs are endlessly churning. Here the gastric juices are never allowed to run a quiet, leisurely course. They are for ever on the jolt. I daresay there are well-ordered establishments where you could serve cheesecake, sausage rolls and plum pudding at every meal without arousing more than a faint hiccup. But in this house stomachs need cosseting if they are to keep up with the strain of violent and emotional living.

Diana And whose fault is that?

Ben Oh, mine, mine, of course, mine—like everything else that goes wrong . . .

Charles enters from outside

Victoria Where were you? Where have you been?

Charles Good heavens—what's the matter with Sophie?

Victoria I looked everywhere—I thought you'd gone.

Diana Overdose.

Charles Intentional?

Diana Yes.

Charles Oh my God.

Victoria I thought you'd gone.

Charles Diana, poor Diana, how awful for you. What can I do to help?

Ben (*to Victoria*) Dance with the left-out ones—take that tray up to Michael. (*Pause*) Satisfied?

Charles (*ignoring him*) When's the doctor coming?

Diana He's not.

Charles *What?*

Diana Ben won't have him.

Charles *Won't?*

Ben (*snarling*) Won't. Won't. Won't.

Diana (*hastily*) Charles, would you like to look at the children? I don't like leaving them.

Ben Why should he look at the children? I'll go.

Diana We'll both go. Victoria, will you take over from me, dear? (*She hands her half of Sophie to Victoria*)

Victoria (*taking it*) Charles will help me.

Charles Of course. (*He takes Ben's side*)

Ben glares at Charles, but Charles ignores him

Diana We won't be long—just have a quick look. (*She looks at Sophie*) You must do better than this, Sophie.

Diana and Ben go out to the house

Victoria looks at Toby. Silence

Victoria (*exasperated*) Toby.

Toby Mm? (*Pause*) Oh. You mean I'm here. Ah. (*Pause. He dismounts*) Better find somewhere else, hadn't I?

Charles Don't go.

Toby gets to the door, then returns for the whisky bottle

Toby My dear chap. Don't let your finer feelings embarrass you.

Toby exits

Charles (*angrily*) I wish you wouldn't talk to Toby like that.
Victoria Where were you?
Charles It makes everything so difficult for me—I won't be able to come here any more if you can't behave better.
Victoria Charles!
Charles Do have a little sense.
Victoria Charles, take me with you.

Pause

Charles Where on earth to?
Victoria *Anywhere* if you're there.
Charles My dear girl, you're behaving very strangely. You can hardly see me as a home-maker? A nest-builder? I've never understood what makes people put two twigs together. You be a sensible girl. Stay with Toby and keep a roof over your head.
Victoria Charles . . .
Charles And stop ordering him about like that. It's ugly.

Silence

Victoria Ben was right. I simply pass the time for you.
Charles What a vulgar way to talk.
Victoria It's true. Just a—a sex object.
Charles Is that a term of abuse? I don't think so. But if you don't like it, the years will mend it. Soon enough.

Silence. They stand still and look at each other

Victoria Oh, get out of my marrow. Get out, get *out*!
Charles Want me to go?
Victoria No. (*Pause*) Want me?
Charles Yes.
Victoria Now?
Charles Yes. But we have other business.
Victoria Damn.
Charles Later.
Victoria Can't we just drop her? She's quite all right now really, you know.
Charles Of course we can't. (*Pause*) Later.

Pause

Victoria Damn Sophie.

They start walking again

Charles Ben was bloody rude this evening. If I didn't think Diana sometimes needed a bit of help I wouldn't stay here.

Silence

Victoria Damn Ben. Damn and blast him. And damn you.

Ben and Diana come in, followed by Toby

There is a loud noise of music until Ben shuts the door. Diana looks at Sophie and stops

Diana Sophie, you're not *still* being silly? (*Pause*) This is no time to be funny. (*Pause*) We're all getting rather cross with you, dear. You're giving us a lot of trouble. I . . . (*She suddenly goes nearer Sophie and looks attentively at her*)
Charles What's the matter?
Ben What's the *matter*?

Panic. They all crowd round Sophie

Diana Look—she's not supporting herself any longer. They're carrying her.
Ben Get her on the table.

They put Sophie on the table

Charles *Why* didn't you get a doctor? This is going to look terrible.
Victoria She's dead.
Toby Of course she isn't dead.
Victoria Oh my God . . .
Charles Mind her head.
Diana Give me a glass. Victoria, give me a glass.

Victoria gives Diana the glass out of her handbag. Diana holds it to Sophie's nostrils. A long silence

Victoria Well?

Silence

Toby Is she——
Victoria —breathing? (*Speaking together*)
Toby —dead?

Ben gives Sophie the kiss of life. Silence. He repeats it four times

Diana There's nothing—nothing there.
Charles (*on Ben's third kiss of life*) Oh my God, it's impossible. What can we do?
Diana (*putting the glass down*) Oh Sophie, Sophie, be sensible.
Victoria Slap her—shake her—throw water over her.

Ben hits Sophie's heart—gives pulse compression. They all gasp

Diana Ben—what are you doing?
Toby He's going to bring her back.
Victoria (*to Toby*) Surely it's—dangerous.
Toby Leave him alone.
Diana Sophie, the children—think of the children.

Victoria Sophie . . .
Toby Come on, Soph, fight, fight—come on back.

Ben gives her the kiss of life again, twice. The others stand frozen. He starts massaging again

Charles She's turning blue.
Victoria Her fingers are blue.
Toby Come *on*! Come *on*! You're still there. Come—*on*! Come—*home*! Fight. Fight.
Diana Oh God, bring her back.
Toby Come—*on*!
Ben The glass.
Victoria (*holding the glass to Sophie*) There's nothing there.
Diana Help. God—help Sophie—Sophie—help—help—God.
Victoria Sophie—the children—think—the children. (*She shouts in Sophie's ear*) Come out of that limbo—come back—come—back . . . (*Her voice fades away*)
Diana Thy will be done. They will be done . . .
Victoria Only if it's to bring her back. Bring back her mind, God, and make her body twitch.
Charles Breathe—breathe . . .

Total silence. Ben goes on massaging. They are all frozen as though about to run a race. The silence is long

Toby (*urgently*) We *want* you back. We want *you* back. (*Silence*) Ben, do something. Do more. You can always do anything. Get her back, Ben. Force her back. You can do it. (*Pause. To Victoria, confidently*) You'll see—he can do anything when he really tries.

Ben goes on massaging. A long silence. Eventually he stands back, panting. Victoria crouches by Sophie. Silence

Ben The glass. The glass.

Victoria holds the glass to Sophie's nostrils. A long silence

Victoria It's—clouding. Look. Look, Diana, look, Charles, look—look at the beautiful clouds. It's life. Only minutes ago there was—nothing. Now—look at that life. (*She embraces Diana*) Life—life—lovely life. (*She holds up the glass again and pulls Diana to look at it*) You see, don't you—how strong it is. Wake up, Sophie, wake up, it's a new world. Do you hear, Sophie? A new world.
Ben She can rest for a few minutes. She'll do.

They all stagger as though drunk. Ben, yawning, puts his head down on the table and seems to go to sleep

Diana Well done, Ben. You did it. Well done.
Toby I knew he could do it. If he wanted to. He can do anything if he wants to.

During the next speech Victoria wanders round the room, unable to stay still. She comes suddenly within Charles's physical orbit and stands rigid. Toby watches as they look at each other, absorbed in each other, sleep-walking

Diana *Ooooh!* (*She gives a long, drawn-out sigh, and stretches*) It was all right, you know. Everything was—marvellous. They all looked so happy. I wish it could go on for ever for them. If only time would stop, and everything else—the music, and the lights, and the dancing—just—flowed on.

Charles and Victoria exit to the house

There is a long silence, then Toby, moving very suddenly, bounds at the clock and wrenches off the minute hand

Toby Then why don't we stop it? What's time ever done for us? Are we to feel grateful for the havoc it's brought us? If it weren't for time, everything would be—like it was. There. How silly it looks. It's—it's—(*waving towards the clock*)—dead.

Diana (*in exasperation, not surprise*) Oh, *Toby* . . .

Toby wrenches off the hour hand

Toby No more minutes. No more hours. It's totally done for. Quite—pathetic. Time—was.

Diana That's the third time since Christmas you've broken the clock.

Toby You don't understand. It hasn't done anything for us. Ever. What's it given us? Marriage. *Marriage.*

Diana It's so hard explaining to Tibbits why the hands keep breaking.

Toby Treachery, blackness, damnation—presents from time, tastefully gift-wrapped. (*Shouting at the clock*) Take them back! Whatever you have to offer, I don't want. You've *nothing* for me.

Diana You've got the horrors again, Toby, and I really can't stand it.

Toby (*shouting into the shadows*) Mrs Eppings! Mrs Eppings! You can come out now. Time's stopped. (*Menacingly*) I know you're there, Mrs Eppings. Why don't you answer? I want to know about those lies. (*Pause*) James! James! Did you hate us, James? (*Pause*) Don't you hear, you can all come out now. (*Pointing to the clock*) It's—dead.

Diana There's no-one there, Toby.

Toby Don't be silly, they're all there. The room's crowded.

Diana They're *buried*, dear. Over there—(*she points vaguely*)—in the churchyard. They're very—contented. They have lovely flowers growing out of them. Snowdrops and so forth. Very nice.

Toby Their mouths are stopped with snowdrops.

Diana And the children do the weeding. They're very good about it.

Toby Crowded—they're all around us. There's no room for a soul to breathe—jostle, jostle, every inch taken. (*Pause*) Gross overcrowding. (*In a matter-of-fact tone*) Slum conditions, really.

Diana (*shaking Ben*) Ben, Toby's got the horrors again.

Toby (*lunging into a dark corner*) I see you!

Diana It's the second time this evening, and it's too much. (*Pause*) Can't we have him dried out or something?

Toby James . . .

Ben (*lifting his head from his hands and looking at Toby*) Is there anything left to dry out?

Diana Of course there is. He doesn't have the horrors all the time. They'll be gone in five minutes.

Silence, while Ben examines Toby, who is looking into dark corners and muttering

Toby Mrs Eppings, Martha, Jenny . . .

Toby exits through the pantry opening

Ben He could be dried out, I suppose. But nothing will bring him back to life if he doesn't want to come. He's doing a Sophie.

Diana Doing a . . . ?

Ben Suicide is what he's up to. He's killing his mind and body because he can't stand the pain.

Diana *What* pain?

Ben Being alive. He always flinched at everything, don't you remember? Finding a dead blackbird in the snow, lack of love, unkindness—growing up. Now he's flinching on a rather larger scale. (*Dispassionately*) I think he's beyond help.

Diana Don't say that, Ben. He's so—*nice*. So loving. He can't be so far gone . . .

Ben (*exploding*) When I think what I meant life in this house to be—and what it is. I meant us all to be so *happy*. A family commune, an answer to the horrors of modern life in a mad world. The family—like a clenched fist—guns pointing outwards.

Diana You were quite right, Ben. Look at the children.

Ben Yes. But what about us? Toby—Sophie—you . . .

Diana Me? I'm perfectly all right.

Ben You've never been all right since Simon jilted you. Twenty years ago.

Silence

Diana My hands have got very rough. I must put some cream on them.

Ben So it's still a green wound. (*Pause*) If only you'd take it out and look at it closely it would become stale, flat and familiar. It would stop eating you. (*Pause*) Forty isn't too old to start growing again. But you must—know—your—demons.

Silence

Diana I saw him. About a year ago.

Ben Where?

Diana In London. He was walking down Bond Street in front of me. I hadn't seen him since—since . . .

Ben What?

Diana He was fat. He'd lost a lot of hair. He looked prosperous. But I felt . . . (*She pauses*)

Ben What did you feel?

Pause

Diana Young. Desperate. (*Silence*) Just—the same. Like I haven't felt for twenty years. Alive. Trembling. Terrified.

Ben Did you speak to him?

Diana *No*. (*Silence*) I went into the Ritz and was sick down the lavatory. (*Silence*) I hadn't—changed, you see. (*Silence*) Don't—undermine me, Ben. Because I love Michael, I love my children, and I'm more than reconciled to life. I enjoy most days. So just—leave it to lie.

Ben stretches out a hand and puts it over hers. Silence

And what about you?

Ben (*after a pause*) I would be all right—I suppose—if when I came home at the week-end I had love. With love you can do anything. But when I arrive on Friday evening, no-one actually has any time for me. And I'm not generous enough—to be happy watching a family going about its own concerns with no thoughts for me. I go back on Monday more tired than when I came down. And I am unfaithful to my wife, not because of the lusts of the flesh, but because I need love . . . No, don't say it. You're right, I haven't found it. Well, *why* can't I get love? What's the matter with me? No, don't tell me that either. If you need love you don't get it. Let your need be total and you'll drive everyone away—they'll *run*. And my need appals my wife, so she—runs. Tonight we've had the longest run yet. Escape from Colditz. But the Gauleiter brought her back. (*Glaring at Sophie*) Snarl, snarl, gloat, gloat. (*Pause*) I saw the greengrocer and his wife out for a walk. They've been married for forty years. He has no hair—no teeth—but they were holding hands. No-one holds my hand. I can neither win love nor grow reconciled to being without it. Can't get used to the idea. (*Urgently*) Tell me how to win love or live without it.

Diana You're surrounded by it.

Ben The dogs get more affection than I do. They're fondled, cherished—who fondles me? (*Bitterly*) And why should anyone?

Diana You're just being sorry for yourself. Now, if you were weak like me . . .

Ben *Weak? You?* My dear Diana. A combination of Joan of Arc, Hercules and Popeye. After Simon left you, you—*built* yourself. What a construction. An impregnable fortress to shelter the rest of us. An ark . . .

Michael enters

Michael (*to Diana, reproachfully*) Had to get my own coffee. *And* bring the cup down. I thought you might come up with a little brandy.

Diana We've been looking after Sophie.

Michael Never mind, never mind. Here now. Get it myself. (*He rummages *for the brandy*) Sophie all hotsy-totsy again, eh? (*To Diana*) If you *really* want to help you can get me a hot water bottle. Sweat this temperature out.

Diana (*resignedly*) Yes, Michael. I'll get it now.

Diana goes out to the house

Michael goes and pours himself a large glass of brandy

Toby appears from the pantry, still looking in dark corners

Michael Doesn't look like one of Toby's better evenings.

Michael exits to the house

As the door is opened, strains of "Good night, sweetheart" are heard

Ben What on earth are they playing that for? It's one of *our* parents' songs. Part of their nostalgia, I suppose, for what they imagine to have been our carefree youth. Before time was. In the olden days.

Toby closes the door and comes forward, glazed and mechanical, and starts singing

Toby "Good night, sweetheart,
Till we meet tomorrow.
Good night, sweetheart,
Sleep will banish sorrow—

Ben But it never does, does it? Wonder if they've noticed.

Toby —Tears and partings
May make us forlorn
But with the dawn
A new day is born . . ."
(*He comes to with a shiver*) Christ. A new day.

Ben Are you with us again?

Toby Only on a temporary basis. Purely temporary, my dear Ben, I assure you.

Ben While you're here you can help me get Sophie into the chair. It's time she sat up.

Ben and Toby help Sophie into a chair

Toby Ben . . .

Ben The one lasting result of this evening's gallimaufry will be permanent injury to my spine.

Toby Ben . . .

Ben What is it?

Toby Tell her you're glad she's back.

Ben What?

Toby Ben . . .

Ben Christ! (*He goes and pours a drink*)

Toby (*after a silence*) What happened, Ben? When did you change? What happened to the child who used to ride Socrates? What happened to all that hope? (*Silence*) You can have Socrates. If you want him so much. I don't want him. I want the boy who used to ride him back. I watch the way you treat Sophie. The child who rode for Erzerum couldn't have treated anyone like you treat her. What happened to him? (*Pause*) Is he dead?

Ben He put away childish things.

Toby Do you remember how we used to dream about being grown up? Panting with eagerness, yearning—for *this*. You so treacherous and unkind that your wife hasn't the heart to go on living. Diana, a heavy-handed matron, never dancing or singing any more. Me—ugh—me . . .

Ben But the children, Toby—*all* our children—they're marvellous.

Toby And are they to end like us? Drunken, frivolous, and middle-aged?

Ben No, they're better than we were.

Toby They're *not* better than we were. Don't you remember? What were we like?

Ben We were like other children.

Toby No.

Silence

Ben What are you on about?

Silence

Toby I wanted you to lead me somewhere. (*Pause*) I always knew you would. (*Pause*) I've always been waiting for you to say—where we were going. What—great enterprise. What new Erzerum. I've been waiting in the wings. Hanging about. (*Pause*) Aren't you going to lead me anywhere? Ever? Nowhere in the world?

Ben Toby, I grew up.

Toby Grew up.

Ben *Someone had to.*

Silence

Toby No Roland. No Oliver. No Erzerum.

Ben That's right.

Toby You should have told me. It's rather late, isn't it, to realize that one's life is built on straw?

Ben It's *not* too late.

Toby Oh, you're strong, Ben. Robust. Nothing's too late for you.

Sophie mutters something

What, Sophie? What did you say?

Ben Probably thanking us brokenly. (*He shouts at Sophie*) Speak up!

Toby Ben!

Ben (*to Sophie*, *exploding*) It's intolerable. We spend a miserable evening bringing you back to your senses, we ruin our backs, our digestions are shot to pieces, and then all you can do is groan. What about a word of thanks? A cheery smile? (*Giving up*) Oh, stick pins in her. (*He goes to the dresser for a drink*)

Toby Ben! Don't. Please don't.

Silence

Ben (*shouting, overwhelmed*) Oh, all right, all *right*. Come back, Sophie, come back—newly born—and love me. *Love me*. I need you to hold my hand when my teeth fall out. I need you to cheer me when I'm unhappy, to understand my needs and support my weakness. I need you to comfort me when the world ignores me, when more able men win the prizes that escape me, when younger men race by me. (*He kneels by Sophie*) You've never felt much passion for me, and now, I suppose, you never will. But we have not got *nothing*. Look around at other marriages and then ask who are we to cry stinking fish. Come back, Sophie. I need you for my wife.

Very slowly, Sophie holds out her hand to Ben. He takes it and kisses it

Sophie I'll—try. (*Pause*) Heaven help us.
Ben Yes. Perhaps. I hope.

Silence

Sophie It was—cold.
Ben What was?
Sophie What?
Ben What was cold?
Sophie I don't know. (*Pause*) I heard—everything you were saying. All the time. But I couldn't—speak. It was—it was . . .
Ben It was what?
Sophie Cold. (*Pause*) Would I have gone on hearing you after—after . . .?
Ben After you were dead.
Sophie Yes.
Ben Abstract speculation of that nature pays few dividends.
Sophie Dividends. (*Pause*) I was wrong, Ben.
Ben Of course you were wrong.
Sophie I don't know what the answer is.
Ben We're going to try. That's what the answer is.
Sophie Not easy.
Ben Of course it's not easy. We're going to have a terrible time.
Toby That's right. Cheer her up.
Ben (*not listening to Toby*) But consider the alternative. And then get down on your knees and pray for strength.

Diana enters

Outside there is the noise of voices and laughter

Diana Come on, Ben, they want to thank you.
Ben Thank me? (*He rises*)
Diana For having them. Oh, *there* you are, Sophie, back at last—really, you gave us quite a fright, you know, you really shouldn't have done it. But we won't say anything more about it.
Sophie I . . .

Diana No, dear, we'll just forget it. We all make mistakes. I did exactly the same thing myself once.

Ben } You . . . { (*Speaking together*)
Toby }

Diana Yes.

Silence

Toby *Diana*—why?

Diana Because I thought there was nothing to live for, of course. That's the usual reason, isn't it? Because death seemed such a good idea. Because I couldn't see in front of me the chance of a single day's happiness. (*Briskly*) I was quite wrong, of course. And so were you. Life is perfectly possible. Come on, Ben, I don't want them all trailing in here to say good-bye.

Ben and Diana go out

Toby *Well.*

Silence. Sophie rises and goes to the sink for a drink of water

Sophie I thought—I thought I knew her.

Toby Sophie . . .

Sophie Mm?

Toby I never knew about Diana. (*To himself*) How *could* she? I never knew—so I couldn't help. I'd like to help you. It won't be easy—you and Ben.

Sophie sits and picks up her pencil and sketch-book

Sophie Don't move . . . My mouth tastes awful.

Toby You'll need an ally. We might sometimes—have a drink together. I'd like someone to have a drink with. We could—talk.

Pause. Sophie draws

Sophie What about?

Toby Oh—candle-snuffers. Elephant guns.

Sophie *Candle*-snuffers?

Toby Anything you like. *Petit point.*

Sophie Why candle-snuffers?

Toby It's not much of an offer. But it's meant as a—bridge.

Sophie A bridge.

Toby A small, delicate, but resilient bridge.

Pause

Sophie I don't know anything about elephant guns.

Toby You would have an ally.

Sophie Or bridges.

Toby I'll play you my old seventy-eights if you like.

Pause

Sophie I'm not at all musical. (*She throws down her pencil*)

Silence

Toby Forget it.

Silence. Sophie looks at Toby. She goes and sits by him

Ben and Diana enter. The door is open, but there is total silence outside. They sit down at the table

Diana Silence. Lovely silence. They've all gone. (*Pause*) Lord, how tired I am. What an evening. *What* an evening. (*Pause*) Where are Charles and Victoria? Why aren't they here?

Pause

Ben Nothing happened.

Diana I haven't seen them for ages. Where are they?

Ben Nothing happened. A few middle-aged people turned on each other. Blamed each other for not being twenty any more. Threatened to leave each other. Realized they would not do better anywhere else. Decided to stay.

Diana I suppose they've gone to bed. Odd, not saying good night.

Ben Some children had a dance and thought the evening—the world—would go on for ever. Nothing happened.

Sophie (*giving an enormous yawn*) Thank you, Toby. I'd like that. (*She yawns*) Elephant guns. (*She puts her head on Toby's shoulder and goes fast asleep*)

Toby looks at her in amazement, then very gently makes her head more comfortable

Ben (*looking at Sophie and Toby*) A few wounds were examined. Some were healing nicely. Others were seen to go deeper. One or two were noticed to be mortal. Nothing happened. (*He goes to the sink*)

Diana Anyhow. The children had a lovely dance.

Ben (*looking out of the window*) Dawn's breaking. Silence, and the dawn breaking. (*He laughs*) Look—come here.

Diana joins him and looks out of the window

Diana Oh!

Toby What?

Diana The children . . .

Toby Haven't they gone home? Perhaps they want breakfast.

Diana No—ours. Oh really, haven't they *any* sense?

Toby Devilled kidneys—kedgeree.

Diana They're dancing on the grass. They've got no shoes on, and they're practically naked. I must go and . . .

Ben Leave them.

Diana But they'll get pneumonia . . .

Ben *Leave them.* (*Restraining her*) It's their morning.

CURTAIN

FURNITURE AND PROPERTY LIST

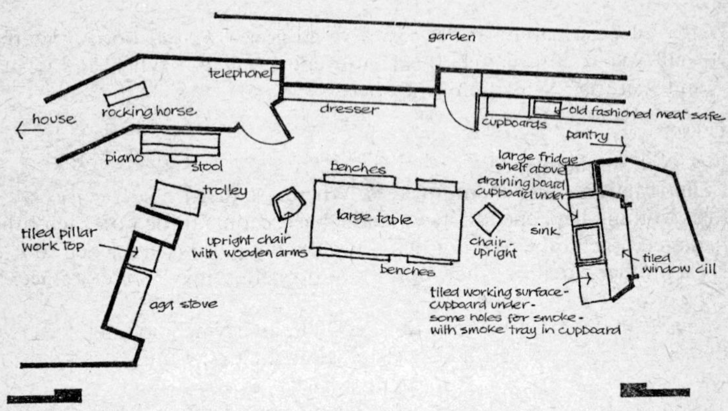

ACT I

On stage: Aga stove. *On it:* kettle of hot water, oven-gloves. *On rail:* tea towel. *On shelf above:* small saucepan, other saucepans as dressing

Tiled work top.

Upright piano. *On it:* music

Piano stool

Dresser. *On shelves:* plates, egg-cups, cruet set, hanging cups, mugs. *On working surface:* 3 cakestands filled with cakes, 2 silver coasters, note-pad and pencil, vase of roses, each with pin attached, small napkin, cutlery tray with spare cutlery, full brandy bottle and goblets, 2 full whisky bottles with tumblers, full water-jug. *In cupboards:* 1930s radio, dressing. *In drawer:* silver-cleaning cloths and gloves

Cupboard. *On it:* 6 french loaves. *In it:* 2 silver candlesticks

Meatsafe. *In it:* wooden box of cheese, open carton of eggs

Refrigerator. *In it:* bowl of mulberries. *On shelf above:* jam in pot, jam-spoon, butter in dish and knife. *Beside it:* **Diana**'s apron on hook

Draining-board: *On it:* wire lettuce-cleaner, plate of watercress, large brown loaf on board with knife, tablespoon, spare cutlery

Sink (practical). *In it:* plastic bowl, soap. *Below it:* 2 dishcloths, waste-bin

Tiled work surface beside sink. *On it:* electric toaster with pre-set slice of burnt toast, smoke effect in cupboard below with holes for escape, and filled kettle, rubber gloves, tea towels

Tiled window-sill above sink. *On it:* "elm tree" picture, bowl of sugar, mops, powders, etc., as dressing

Large kitchen table. *On it:* 4 large trays with plates of food covered with napkins (2 trays of ham—one piece of "real" ham, 1 tray of chicken, 1 tray of duck), 1 large plate of chicken covered with napkin, 3 large plates of decorated rice. *In drawers:* car key, silver spoons and forks, chamois cloths, teaspoon, carving-knife. *Under table:* 1 bone
4 benches
1 small kitchen chair
1 kitchen chair with arms
2-tier trolley. *On it:* large iced cake, jellies, blancmanges on plates
On wall above piano: clock with detachable hands, set at 10.30 p.m.
In hallway: black telephone on shelf
On main door: hook with apron and shopping bags

Off stage: Rocking-horse **(Ben, Toby)**
Tray with olive oil, vinegar, pepper-grinder, bowl, tablespoon **(Sophie)**
Half lemon and squeezer **(Diana)**
2 lettuces **(Diana)**
Sketch-book and pencil **(Sophie)**
Several letters and catalogues—envelopes splashed slightly with paint **(Ben)**

Personal: **Ben:** handkerchief, watch
Toby: handkerchief, watch

ACT II

Strike: Bread, lettuce, wire cleaner
All dirty crockery and glasses

Set: Butter dish and jampot back on shelf
Bread board on draining-board
Full coffee-pot on tiled working surface at sink
4 mugs by coffee-pot
Sketch-book and pencil by coffee things
Diana's bag, with mirror in it, on dresser
Both doors closed
Benches and chairs well under table (except one downstage bench) to make room for walk-round

LIGHTING PLOT

Property fittings required: 2 kitchen pendants
Interior. A kitchen. The same scene throughout

ACT I. Late evening

To open: Pendants on. Sunset effect outside

Cue 1 **Ben:** "... packed with young people." (Page 2)
Fade sunset to dark

ACT II. Night

To open: As close of Act I

Cue 2 **Ben:** "Nothing happened." (Page 57)
Bring up light slowly outside to suggest dawn

EFFECTS PLOT

ACT I

Cue 1 **Toby:** "... dancing a toe short." (Page 23)
Telephone rings

Cue 2 **Toby:** "KEEP BRITAIN TIDY." (Page 23)
Noise of guests arriving

Cue 3 **Charles** enters (Page 26)
Loud music until door closes. From now and throughout the Act, whenever the door is open, music and party noises are heard

ACT II

Cue 4 **Diana** exits to the house (Page 39)
Party noises and music as in previous Act, whenever the door is open, until the end of the dance

Cue 5 **Michael:** "... Toby's better evenings." (Page 53)
Party music—"Good night, Sweetheart", continue until door closes

Cue 6 **Diana** enters (Page 55)
Noise of voices and laughter from departing guests, until door closes